THE COUNTRYSIDE ~
RANDOM GLEANINGS

THE COUNTRYSIDE ~ RANDOM GLEANINGS

by THE COUNTRYMAN
RALPH WHITLOCK

L_G The Gavin Press

First Edition 1982

© 1982 Ralph Whitlock
© 1982 Illustrations The Gavin Press Limited

Published by The Gavin Press Limited, 36, Fore Street, Evershot, Dorchester, Dorset.

ISBN 0 905868 07 2

Typeset by Photosetting & Secretarial Services Ltd., Yeovil, Somerset.
Printed in Great Britain by The Dorset Press, Dorchester, Dorset.

CONTENTS

Illustrations by Harriet Forrester

INTRODUCTION

I am often asked how I came to start writing The Countryside column in the *Western Gazette* and its associated papers. Perhaps now, on the eve of that column's fiftieth anniversary, is the time to reveal all.

The village in which I was reared had been from time immemorial the scene of a struggle for existence by a community of small farmers – peasant farmers. Crouched in the bottom of a waterless chalk valley on the edge of Salisbury Plain, it wallowed in an isolation hardly imaginable today. Until 1938 it had no electricity, no piped water supply and no telephones. Almost every winter the rutted, gritty roads were blocked by snow for days or weeks, an event so familiar that it was taken for granted. The carrier's cart, by which I can remember travelling, made the journey to Salisbury twice a week, taking two-and-a-half hours to cover six miles. Most passengers, except invalids and pregnant women, had to get out and walk up the hills, and able-bodied men were expected to push. Many villagers went to town only twice a year – the first time just before Easter, the second to attend Salisbury Fair in October.

Ours was a virtually self-sufficient and highly introverted society. Nearly everyone gained a livelihood within the village boundaries, mostly on the farms though some as carpenters, builders, blacksmiths and underwood workers. The only exception was a schoolmaster, pioneer of all commuters, who cycled to town daily.

To the north the village fields merged with the open downland which then extended with hardly a break some thirty miles or so to Warminster. Its short turf gave sustenance to millions of rabbits and little else. To south, east and west we were hemmed in by great woodlands the far sides of which joined up with the New Forest. It was frontier country, ideally designed for an incipient naturalist.

After cycling, in my turn, to school in Salisbury daily for four years and taking the Oxford School Certificate exams (the equivalent of the present "O" levels) with some distinction I came home in the summer of 1930 and was immediately engulfed, as usual, by the harvest. It happened every summer, but this year when September came I did not return to school. I would have liked to. I wanted to sample life in the sixth form and then go on to college, but this year was the nadir of the Depression, and there were two younger children in the family to be educated.

For the next few years my education was in the practical arts of the farm. I learned how to milk by hand, to plough with horses, to make a rick and thatch it, to lay a hedge, to rear and pluck poultry, to kill a pig and cut it up, to make butter, to flat-hoe and single turnips, to pollard a tree and to acquire reasonable skill in dozens of other basic tasks which are now not of the slightest use to me. For all this work my father could afford to pay me ... nothing! It was, as I said, the time of the Great Depression. Nobody had any money. The taxman did not then know that our village existed; there was nothing there for him.

Our cash needs were few, living as we did on home-grown vegetables, home-produced eggs and butter and easily caught rabbits. To cater for mine I shot and snared rabbits, kept pens of pure-bred hens (selling sittings of eggs for hatching), bred budgerigars and guinea-pigs, and cut beanrods and peasticks. My father sold these commodities for me in Salisbury. Occasionally the thought occurred to me that there must be easier ways of earning pocket-money. In one of these introspective moods I suddenly realised that the local papers were printing no news from our village. In their pages I read reports of fetes, carnivals, whist drives, socials, births, marriages and deaths from neighbouring parishes, but nothing from ours.

Enquiring further, I learned that three weekly papers had a local circulation – the *Western Gazette* and two Salisbury papers – and that each paid a halfpenny a line for village news. Within a few weeks I persuaded all three to appoint me official reporter for our village, a scoop which enabled me, by the use of carbon paper, to earn a penny-halfpenny a line.

Not long afterwards readers of the three papers began to express surprise at the number and variety of events reported for our parish. What a lively and progressive place this remote village must be! Never a week went by without something noteworthy happening – otherwise I earned no pocket-money!

When the human inhabitants failed me I turned to the wild ones. The first swallows and the first primroses were always good for a few lines. I reported the damage wrought by fallow deer on our mangolds, the autumn flocking of stone curlew (then quite common), the arrival of winter waterfowl on the lake a few miles away, the nesting of woodcock and nightjars, the discovery of a colony of the spiked star of Bethlehem. As all these notes were duly printed and paid for (at the same rate) it seemed a good idea to suggest a regular countryside article. The Editor of the *Western Gazette* agreed.

So, in February, 1932, I started to write my weekly Country-side article, and I have done so every week since. For fifty years.

My life since then has been more eventful than I could have foreseen. I have been a farmer and am now no longer a farmer. I have been a radio and television personality (as the expression goes) though have done comparatively little in either medium during the past few years. For seventeen years I had my own radio programme on the BBC's Children's Hour – Cowleaze Farm. For over thirty years I was sometimes Farming Correspondent, sometimes Farming Editor, of *The Field*. I spent five years travelling extensively, as agricultural consultant to a world-wide charity, in Africa, India, Europe, America and the Caribbean countries and found myself lecturing or broadcasting in most of them. To date I have had rather more than seventy books published. Sometimes I have been comparatively affluent, sometimes decidedly impecunious; sometimes enjoying good health, sometimes not; sometimes buoyant, sometimes depres-sed; – up and down like a seesaw. And through it all I have sat down once a week, often in bizarre surroundings, to jot down a few pages of notes on the countryside.

Notes much like those I started with, in 1932. Notes on the cycle of the seasons; on the state of the harvest; on the occurrence of rare storm-driven migrant birds; on the uncanny behaviour of domestic animals; on the techniques of half-forgotten crafts; on country folk I have known; on folk-lore and local history. Sometimes I discuss controversial topics. Sometimes I reminisce. Sometimes I philosophise. When I hear a good country yarn I cannot resist passing it on. As, for instance, the one I heard many years ago when the Milk Marketing Board was beginning its career. This smallholder was surprised one morning by an early visit from the milk inspector. 'Bain't hardly ready for ee yet,' he said. 'Shan't be a tick, though. Thee wait till I strains this yer bucket of milk.' With that, he pulled the front of his shirt out of his trousers, strained it over the top of the milk churn and poured the milk through it! And later he was puzzled about why he lost his licence.

Writing my weekly article now occupies about one evening a week, though thoughts about it are with me all the time. As often as not my readers write it for me. A letter gives a cue for a new topic; I start it, and more letters flow in. Readers write, they phone; they call at my door with specimens; they accost me in the streets and in shops and offices. That way I have made dozens, even hundreds, of friends. Writing this weekly column gives me, I think, as much pleasure as anything I have ever done.

And now a kindly publisher, Philip Snowden, whose namesake was, as readers of my own generation will remember, once Chancellor of the Exchequer, has invited me to compile a Countryside miscellany. A collection of my writings for fireside reading. What a task! How to select from the accumulation of a lifetime? From over two million words!

My publisher has lightened the task ...

My father, a notable practitioner in the art of public speaking, was invited to address a meeting when in his late 70s. 'You may think,' he told his audience, 'that this is the first time I have been here, but you would be wrong. I came here once before – forty years ago!' 'That must have been a good speech,' he went on, 'to have lasted you forty years. But I'll assure you of one thing, if you leave it for another forty years before you ask me again, I shan't come!'

This is not so with me, for my publisher has promised that, provided this book meets with an adequate reception, we will have another one next year. And another in the year after that. So I can make a more or less random selection, leaving some of the best bits for next time!

Ah well, what is it that Browning says?
    'Grow old along with me,
      The best is yet to be ...'
I think he was right. In all those fifty years I have never been stuck for things to write about, and I feel sure that some of the most interesting and exciting and profound events have still to happen in the countryside. There will always be something new, and I am looking forward to being on hand to report and comment on them for a long time to come. The windows of my heart are still wide open to the singing of birds, the beating of butterflies' wings, the rustle of ripening corn, the scent of freshly-turned soil, the gusting winds of heaven.

Though fifty years is a long time I understand it is not enough to qualify for an entry in *The Guinness Book of Records*. But sixty years may be. So, on to the Diamond Jubilee!

RALPH WHITLOCK
February 1982

IN THE SEASONS OF THE YEAR

Harvest Home & Hymn Singing

(Written in September, 1977)

The more remote the harvest becomes from the everyday life of most people, the greater, it seems, the popularity of harvest festivals, not only the secular harvest homes and suppers but the church services when we joyfully sing,

'All is safely gathered in
Ere the winter-storms begin,'

most of us not having been involved in a corn harvest for years. Indeed, harvest festivals are one of the three services in the year when churches can expect a full congregation, the others being, hopefully, Easter and Christmas. Clergymen have told me that they welcome these special occasions, as it gives them the chance to see members of their flock who otherwise enter the church doors only for baptisms, weddings and funerals. Still, church-going is not necessarily a criterion of Christian behaviour. In England we cannot match the religious enthusiasm that I saw exhibited at a church in Los Angeles one Easter, where three policemen were needed to control the traffic and direct cars to parking places and where the collections for the day amounted to over £2,500 (and that in 1965!) but I have not noticed that the Americans are any more God-fearing than we are.

And what slaves to the calendar we are! The other day someone asked me if I would be willing to give a talk to a certain society, and I said that in principle I would. The next week he told me regretfully that he had found that the secretary had just finished making out the programme to September, 1978, so it would have to wait till after then. So the proposition would be that I commit myself to standing up and addressing an audience, on a subject which by then I may have lost interest in, 400 to 500 days from now. And I dare say that some super-efficient churches have already fixed the date of their 1978 harvest festivals, on the basis of fitting in with other autumn events, regardless of whether next year's harvest is early or late. Well, I suppose it is all part of this ultra-regimented age, when one cannot go into a shop and buy a tube of toothpaste without someone making a paper record of the transaction, but we miss a lot of the joy of spontaneity. What we are required to do is to produce emotions to order, and no more so than in the churches, where our mood is expected to be cosily optimistic at Christmas, gloomy in Lent, triumphant at Easter and thankful at harvest festival time. What a contrast with old-time harvest rejoicings, when, after six or eight weeks of incessant had labour in the harvest fields, at last the final sheaf was hoisted on to the waggon! What a shout of triumph went up! Hats were thrown into the air, green boughs were torn down to decorate the waggon which bore the last sheaves homeward, the whole company of harvesters piled on to the load and sang all the way home. And in the feast that followed there was no need to go easy on the ale or cider, for there was no more harvesting to be tackled next day.

No doubt it was partly as a corrective to the more uninhibited aspects of the proceedings that Rev. R. S. Hawker, the vicar of

Morwenstow in Cornwall, arranged the first church harvest festival in 1843. It can come as a shock to realise that harvest festivals in their present form are of such recent origin. But we need only to look at the familiar harvest hymns to realize that nearly all of them were written after about 1850. 'Come, ye thankful people, come', 'To Thee, O Lord, our hearts we raise', 'Now the year is crowned with blessing', 'Praise, O praise, our God and King', 'O Lord of heaven and earth and sea', and the Manx fishermen's hymn, all fall into that category, and 'We plough the fields and scatter' was translated in the same period, though originally a somewhat older German hymn. They are not age-old expressions of rejoicing.

But then, hymn singing in church is itself a fairly recent development, though probably a revival of an early Christian custom. Did you know that until about 1820 it was illegal to sing hymns in Anglican churches (though the rule was not strictly observed)? I gleaned that fact from a recently published book, *Christianity in Somerset*, by Dr. Robert Dunning, which I have just been reading and which has largely prompted these thoughts. Not only hymns but other sorts of singing were frowned upon. Dr. Dunning quotes Parson Woodforde, the diarist of Babcary, who in 1769 fell out with the Singers of Castle Cary because 'they had the impudence to sing the responses' when he took a service there.

Hymns Ancient and Modern first came out in 1860 and then apparently as a result of private enterprise, for two Somerset parsons, the vicars of North Curry and Shepton Beauchamp, are mentioned among the proprietors. Hymn singing, of course, owed its popularity to the Methodist revival in the second half of the eighteenth century, John Wesley producing his *Collection of Hymns* in 1779. Charles Wesley wrote about six thousand hymns, and John translated a lot of German ones.

As the habit of hymn-singing spread from the Nonconformist churches to the Anglican, individual churches compiled their own hymnals. They continued to do so long after *Hymns Ancient and Modern* had become available. The Somerset village of Ashbrittle published its own collection in 1877, and the Rev. Godfrey Thring, rector of Alford, not only produced his *Hymns and Sacred Lyrics* in 1874 but also wrote a number of hymns for it. Some of his hymns are now in common use; they include 'From the eastern mountains', 'Fierce raged the tempest o'er the deep' and 'Saviour, blessed Saviour, listen while we sing'.

The new demand for hymns also produced tune-writers. Among the tunes from Somerset musicians which have survived are the familiar one to 'Angel voices', composed by Dr. Edwin Monk who was born at Frome, and the one to 'Jerusalem the golden' by Colonel A. Ewing, who died at Taunton. Dr. Dunning says that the Somerset village of Goathurst possessed tunes, most of them evidently composed locally, for 200 hymns and 44 anthems, 'some of them of a respectable standard'. Thomas Shoel of Montacute was another composer whose work was frequently used locally.

In the Wiltshire village chapels of my boyhood days hymns from the *Methodist Hymn Book* (then the *Wesleyan Methodist Hymn Book*) were used on Sundays, but for weeknight meetings other collections were preferred, notably *Sankeys* and a collection known as *Alexanders*, probably because they had rousing tunes with choruses! For special occasions collections of hymns and anthems were obtained from certain specialist publishing firms in Yorkshire, which presumably still flourish. When attending church (the United Church of Canada) on my recent visit to British Columbia I found that the hymns, of which I knew very few, resembled the *Sankey* collection more than the Anglican and Methodist ones with which I am familiar.

The antipathy towards hymn singing was not confined to Anglicans in the seventeenth and eighteenth centuries. The Puritans indulged in quite a bit of organ-smashing. They thought organ music was out of place at religious services. So many of the organs which survived the Reformation were destroyed by order of the Parliament of 1644. Any singing in church for the next hundred years or so was usually to other instruments, many of them locally made. Barrel organs were installed in some churches, as at Muchelney where I heard one being played at Easter. But gradually organs replaced other instruments, and many of these too, in the early days, were home-made. Examples may still be found in many West Country villages, by those who take the trouble to search.

Incidentally, Dr. Dunning's book shows that staying away from church is not a modern phenomenon. 'At a census taken in 1851, in the middle of the so-called age of church-going, just over 28% of the people of Somerset attended either a church or chapel on the morning of March 30th, and only 18.5% went to an Anglican church.'

Samhain and Punkie Night

My two-year-old grandson in British Columbia was initiated into the joys of Hallowe'en. With his mother and a host of other small kids and their parents he went trotting around the streets of their little town, carrying his pail and knocking at the doors for 'tuck and treat'. He was, says his mother, dressed up as a lady, with a wig and dress and a blanket over his shoulders. When someone answered the door he presented his little bucket and managed to say, 'Tuck or treat', being rewarded with a handful of sweets, or, as they call them in Canada, 'candies'. At that age, of course, he soon grew tired and so was carried home to watch fireworks before bed.

So, on the far side of the world, the old Hallowe'en traditions are carried on, more extensively than in England. When one of my daughters was living in the United States Hallowe'en was an occasion of considerable festivity, with fancy-dress parties, barbecues, coloured lanterns and pumpkin pies. The trouble with Hallowe'en in England is that it has got itself mixed up with Bonfire Night on November 5th, to which most of the associated customs have been transferred. Guy Fawkes, naturally, has little interest for America or Canada, except perhaps to prompt a slight passing regret that he didn't succeed in his attempt to blow up the British Houses of Parliament (!), so the older festival holds unrivalled sway.

Hallowe'en is the old Celtic Samhain – one of the ancient quarter days. It has its origins in a pastoral festival, pre-dating agriculture. On a date corresponding to November 1st the herdsmen who were our ancestors met in a great tribal gathering and took stock of their flocks and herds. The surplus, for whom there would be insufficient food in the coming winter, were slaughtered and salted down: the ewes were mated for next year's lamb crop; and a gargantuan feast was enjoyed around blazing bonfires. The fires, in which in early days undoubtedly sacrifices were consumed, served the additional purpose of reminding the gods to restore the earth to life after the impending winter sleep.

In accordance with its usual practice, the Christian Church adopted and adapted what it could not suppress or ignore, so in due course Samhain became All Saints' Day. Good Christians were bidden to remember the saints 'who from their labours rest', and in the Middle Ages prayers were also said, around the November bonfires, for souls who were still in Purgatory. But old customs die hard. When the new religion confiscated All Saints' Day the old religion switched its celebrations to All Saints' Eve, October 31st – Hallowe'en. On that day witches, ghosts and all the ancient forces of the supernatural prevailed, and devout Christians stayed indoors, with hag-stones and horse-shoes over the lintels and with chimneys blocked, to keep the witches at bay.

A few places in England, chiefly in the West Country, still keep up at least some of the Hallowe'en customs on the correct date instead of on November 5th. One Hallowe'en I dropped in at the village of Hinton St. George, near Crewkerne, Somerset, for the Punkie Night celebrations. Chief feature of the festivities was a procession by the village children, bearing 'turnip' lanterns. The 'turnips' were, in most instances, mangolds, though in a few, pumpkins, hollowed out to hold a candle and carved into grotesque features. They were carried in procession around the village behind a trailer on which a Punkie King and Queen, with their attendants, sat in state. As they walked the children chanted,

> 'It's Punkie Night tonight,
> It's Punkie Night tonight,
> Adam and Eve, they won't believe
> Tis Punkie Night tonight.

> 'It's Punkie Night tonight,
> It's Punkie Night tonight,
> Gie us a candle, gie us a light,
> It's Punkie Night tonight."

The 50 to 75 lanterns were later judged in the village hall, prizes being awarded for the prettiest, the most grotesque and so on, and the King and Queen were crowned with proper ceremony. 'Punkie' is said to be derived from 'pumpkin'.

It is fair to state that some of the organisers state that Hinton's Punkie Night has nothing to do with Hallowe'en. They maintain that it marks the date of the long defunct Chiselborough Fair (Chiselborough being a neighbouring village), which was held on the last Thursday in October, and tell a story of how the men of Hinton went to the Fair, got drunk and were late coming home.

Their wives became worried, especially as the men had to cross a ford through a stream, so they scooped out lanterns from mangolds, and perhaps from pumpkins, and then went around the village begging for candles or money to go in search of their menfolk! Well, it's a good local yarn, which seems to account logically for the old custom (which, incidentally, was revived and 'commercialised' in the 1940s to raise money for a village hall and playing field), and it might hold water if 'punkies' were confined to Hinton and a few adjacent villages.

But when I was a boy in the 1920s in south Wiltshire we spent the week before Bonfire Night carving mangold lanterns, though we did not call them 'punkies'. So did my father when he was a boy in the 1880s. And so do children now. And pumpkin lanterns are a feature of Hallowe'en celebrations right across the continent of America.

November 5th in my boyhood days had all the characteristics of old-time Hallowe'en. We had not private but a public village bonfire on the hill overlooking the village. We tried or pretended to scare people with our lantern masks. We burnt a guy. Then, as the fire burned low, we went on the rampage.

There was a general belief that on that night we were outside the law.

'The policeman can't touch you for anything you do on Bonfire Night,' we told each other, and we half-believed it. It was a belief directly descended from the postulate that on Hallowe'en the ordinary laws of men and of nature were suspended and the supernatural was supreme.

So we purloined besoms, dipped them in tar, set them alight and ran about, fighting battles with these burning torches as weapons. We took garden gates off hinges and raided apple-lofts. On one occasion a householder's wood-pile was dismantled and the faggots used to build a barrier across the village street. We used fizzing carbide tins as home-made bombs.

Our elders stayed indoors, regarding our excesses with tolerance. They had done just the same sort of things in their youth. No carbide tins in that generation, but my father did tell me once of how the village smithy was nearly wrecked by boys experimenting with gunpowder, a muzzle-loading gun and the anvil one Bonfire Night.

Lewes in Sussex was once notorious for its Bonfire Night festivities, when blazing tar-barrels were rolled down the streets and bonfire parties developed into rowdyism. The bonfires are still held, but those responsible for them themselves maintain reasonable order. At one time the Lewes, like other celebrations, had an anti-Catholic flavour, and an eighteenth century banner bearing the slogan 'No Popery' is still in existence. But it would be mistaken to suppose that the festival had its origins either with Guy Fawkes or with the Reformation. It is far, far older.

So the witches still have their day, or rather, their night, and the observances of the old pagan religion of Britain, though disguised and metamorphosed, are still honoured. Little Canadians with their pails knock at doors to demand 'tuck and treat' just as, according to an old document, 'Irish peasants used to assemble with sticks and clubs, going from house to house collecting money, breadcake, butter, cheese and eggs for the feast ... the good women are employed in making griddle cakes and candles; these last are sent from house to house and are lighted up on the next day, Samhain, before which they pray for the departed soul of the donor.' And Somerset and Wiltshire children parade, as ever, with their bogey masks.

A Witch's Ladder

On Hallowe'en some children came to our door wearing grotesque masks and reciting a rhyme about witches – a rhyme which unfortunately I couldn't catch. We admired their enterprise and so gave them some money for their guy or fireworks.

The visit reminded me of a query put to me some time ago – what was a witch's ladder? It consisted of a cord in which a series of knots were tied at regular intervals, and in each knot a fowl's feather. I gather that as each feather was tied in the witch pronounced a curse on the person to whom she wished evil. In the past such 'ladders' have been found in recesses in churches.

Christmas

Christmasses are for families and for memories. They are a time of wonderment for children, at which parents and other adults conspire to introduce the youngsters to a magic world in which golden balls and glittering tinsel grow on fir trees, and a benevolent old gentleman in white beard and red dressing-gown sails across the night sky in a reindeer-drawn sledge and comes down impossible chimneys, bearing presents, and we venture bravely out on a frosty, starlit night to sing carols about a haunting event of long ago and far away, and all things are possible.

So, when our children are grown up and have left the nest, at Christmas we seek their company again and re-live our youth with our grandchildren. Or, if they are inaccessible, we surround ourselves with as many of the trappings of Christmas as possible and indulge in memories.

I enjoyed so many happy Christmasses when a boy. I can visualise now the Christmas tree in the 'front room', set against the round table and its thick Victorian table-cloth, piled with presents for my brother and sister and myself ... though we had already opened one lot from the pillow-cases at the foot of our beds. We had coloured wax candles on the tree in those days, not fairy lights, but the other accessories were much the same as we shall be enjoying this year ... turkey, Christmas pudding, an iced Christmas cake, crackers (aren't they a waste of money!), new card games to play, holly decorations wedged along the tops of the pictures on the walls, a bunch of mistletoe hanging over a strategic door. My stock presents, I remember, used to be a 'Wonder book' and another set of Meccano. In the evening we played parlour games, and my father always produced a big box of indoor fireworks, although these were usually reserved for Boxing Night, when a houseful of other children came in for a party.

In 1941 I remember thinking that this year my daughter, who had been born on the first anniversary of the outbreak of war, in 1940, would be old enough to appreciate Christmas, so we would be able to have a Christmas tree and presents and everything, just like we used to at my old home. Thirty-five years later we had a family party on the same lines at her home in Bournemouth, but the next year she was back with her American family in California, and my son, with two small children, was sharing Christmas with his Canadian in-laws in Vancouver. We ourselves were with our one daughter still on English soil, in her home not far from where we were born. And, in a house well populated with children, it was very much the same as the other Christmasses we remember.

So the years pass and yet repeat themselves, and I suppose it is trite to say that Christmasses seem to come around more quickly. I know why that is. When I was four, which is about as far back as I can remember, a year was a quarter of my whole life. It was an almost endless expanse of time. The cycle of the seasons was new to me. I had no previous knowledge of the snow and icicles of winter, the expanding of green leaves and golden flowers in spring, the ripening of wheat in summer or the apple harvest in autumn. Each experience came as a surprise. I was just getting to know the world into which I had been born.

But now I know it well, and a year is only one-sixtieth part of my experience. No wonder it passes more quickly.

There is, however, another way of looking at this. I sit in my study on a cold but sunny December afternoon, watching the stone garden wall steaming as the frost evaporates but knowing that on the back lawn, shaded from the sun, the frost is still white and crisp. It is a vivid, fleeting moment. When you read my account of it, the experience will be the past, such as much as the battle of Waterloo is in the past. Your sitting down to read this book is, for me at this moment, an event in the future, though I can assume that it will happen. So all, except a moment less than the tick of the second hand of the clock, is either memory or prevision.

Now I have shut my eyes. I am looking at a field of standing wheat, ripe for harvester. The sky is a brassy blue, and the scent of honeysuckle hangs heavy on the airless heat. Poppies are standing listlessly around the field borders. A solitary yellow hammer wheezes its tuneless song from a wild rose bush on which the hips are beginning to turn red. I have in my hands a scythe, with which I am going to cut a swathe around the margin of the wheat-field, to allow the binder to pass.

All is as clear and real as the frost vapour and the bare branches of the beech trees which I see when I open my eyes again. I have lived through and helped with so many harvests that every detail of sight, sound, scent and touch is as vivid as if I were in the harvest-field now. This particular harvest I am seeing through memory's eye is an actual one. I was there. I can identify the field. But I cannot give a label to the year.

Can you, with most of your memories? I think not. Traumatic events, whether pleasant or disastrous, can be fitted into place against the background of history. We can remember the date of our marriage (or if we cannot our wives soon remind us!), the dates of our children's birthdays, the dates of our parents' deaths, and so on. But the pageant of the seasons is different. I can remember, as clearly as if it were yesterday, picking primroses and violets and wood anemones down the overgrown lane that leads to the copse, but I have no idea which year it was. Probably at some time in the early 1920s. But it doesn't really matter.

For summer is now summer, and not a slice out of one particular year. Summer was endless when I was four, but it is almost so now. For, instead of consisting of ninety days, as in the year that is past, it has expanded to sixty times ninety, – 5,400 days, which is a long time. No wonder I can remember the details of it so well. Daffodils bloom not for one month but for sixty; Christmas lasts not for three days but for a hundred-and-eighty. That is the way that memory works when one is over sixty. And that is how we can enjoy roses in December ...

Some few years ago I composed some verses for our Christmas cards. Now all those Christmas cards have gone, and I have lost the copy of the verses, so I have to start all over again, making up again bits to fill in where my memory fails. But I do it because it seems just the sort of thing I like to say at Christmas.

'When icicles hang vrum the eaves,
    An' night creeps in at half-past dree,
    We draws our chair up be the vire
    An' treats oursel's to toast ver tea.

'Then, when the tea be cleared away,
    An' all our light be log-vire's gleam,
    Wi' memory we zits awhile
    And, as we zits, so we do dream

'Of vrens we hopes to zee agen,
    Who lives their lives both var and near,
    An' we do warmly wish 'em then
    Bright Christmas and a Brave New Year.'

Who Needs a Calendar?

On December 21st, having reminded myself that it was the shortest day of the year, I turned up a selection of books on ancient stone circles and other prehistoric monuments, of which Stonehenge is the outstanding example. One of the latest theories is that Stonehenge served as a giant computer, used in relation to the calendar, and antiquarians seem to set great store on the alleged efforts of primitive men to work out an efficient calendar.

But why? I can understand that a powerful gang of priests world find it very advantageous to be able to predict eclipses, but the return of spring? ... No, I don't think so. Book after book, I find, repeats the theory that a calendar was needed to enable the wise men of the tribe to tell the peasants when to sow and get busy with other agricultural tasks. I don't believe it. Supposing we were suddenly to lose our calendars and all aids to recording the passage of time, would we be at a loss to know when spring had arrived and when it was time to sow barley and cabbages? No, we would not. I fear that once again we countrymen have been under-rated, by academicians sitting among their books when they would have done better to go out and talk with their gardeners.

The Parish Lantern

A South Devon reader sent me a delightful little collection of Devonshire dialect words gathered locally. The words had been put into sentences, to illustrate their uses, and I quote the final paragraph:-

'So 'tis up the wooden-lane and into blanket land (upstairs to bed). 'Tis small wonder you're feeling like that if you've really made yourself "knowsy' (knowledgeable) about all these sayings. So now you'd best be getting along and "straming-on-avore" (striding out), for 'tis a bit of a "jant" (arduous walk) and already 'tis getting "dimpsey" (twilight) and soon be "drapping dark" (dusk) – or you'll find yerselves traipsing home-along by the light of the "Parish Lantern" (the moon).'

Some of these expressions are pure Devonshire, but most of them are widely known throughout Wessex. But when not long ago I referred, quite without premeditation, to the light of the Parish Lantern, some younger folk didn't know what I meant.

The booklet quoted an expression I hadn't heard for a long time. On asking the time an enquirer was told, 'Tis upright the hour', meaning the minute hand is pointing to twelve. And have you ever heard of a farm worker 'tormenting' the land, with a cultivator?

On the subject of country sayings, an old friend reminded me of a poacher's comment on the lengthening of the days as winter progresses:-

'You know 'tis the end of January when you can see to shoot a pheasant out of a tree against the sky at five o'clock.'

It is a pretty accurate observation.

Another countryman assured me that there would be snow at Easter if the sun was visible on Candlemas Day. Without discussing whether or not that has any truth in it (probably not), I wonder whether, apart from a few weather sayings such as this, Candlemas Day means anything today, apart, that is, from Roman Catholic churches. According to the ancient church calendar, Candlemas Day, February 2nd, is the Feast of the Purification, when candles were (or are) blessed and given to the congregation, but for most of England the custom died at the Reformation. Before Christian times it was a pagan feast, for both Romans and the Celts; for the latter it was a quarter day, Imbolc, and in some way connected with the lambing season.

The Candlemas saying most familiar to me is the good old agricultural warning,

'On your farm at Candlemas Day
Should be half the straw and two-thirds of the hay.'
Meaning that the hardest and hungriest times are yet to come.

Spring must follow Winter

It cheered me considerably one morning in February to see the cock chaffinch that has been frequenting our bird table all the winter singing merrily from his perch on an apple bough. He was in splendid spring plumage, too, like a posse of seven drake mallards which I saw parading on the snow-covered shore of the little river at Nunney in the previous week. Even in the watery, weak sunshine of a hazy afternoon their glossy green plumage scintillated as though it had been polished by some particularly conscientious housewife. Under the tree where the chaffinch was singing snowdrops were already showing white, and a blackbird was watching the singing bird contemplatively, as though he were already thinking of tuning up.

Early in the 1970s I spent the whole winter in Africa, dropping in at Malaga, Spain, on the return journey to spend a fortnight with one of my daughters who was then living there; and eventually I arrived home at Easter. Africa was, of course, summer all the time, but southern Spain had arrived at a season which compared best with late May. Orchids and clover were in flower, the trees had expanded their leaves, and the air was filled with swallows, swifts and the hordes of insects on which they were feeding. Back in England the weather was still chilly and people were welcoming the first meagre and reluctant signs of spring – the early celandines, the first violets, a solitary chiffchaff surprised at its own temerity in coming north so early.

After the warmth and exuberance of warmer climates, it all seemed rather trivial. We couldn't get excited about looking for the first primrose. Our main preoccupation was to keep warm. And it was then we realised that to appreciate an English spring you first had to live through an English winter.

I used to think, in a youthful and romantic phase, that I would like once during my life to spend a winter in the Canadian north, just to experience the exhilaration of watching the ice break up, seeing the rapid thaw of spring and watching the short-lived flowers expand and the myriads of migrating birds return from the south. It must be quite dramatic. But now, having lived in lands where there is no winter, I have come to appreciate that here in England I have been enjoying these experiences, admittedly in a relatively mild form, all my life.

So this year I am enjoying as much as ever I did looking for the first signs that winter is ending and that another summer is on the way. And I was particularly delighted the other day to find, on visiting my devastated garden, some rows of broad beans which I had planted last November thrusting an inch or two of strong, creamy-white shoots above the frosty soil. Amid the wreckage of my winter greens they were as welcome as the first swallow.

The Springs

After the unprecedented summer drought of 1976 it seemed almost incredible that in early March in the chalk country springs were rising in places which had been dry for the past ten or twenty years, but even Tilshead, high on Salisbury Plain, had its floods. These were not river floods or floods caused by melting snow but the overflow from saturated chalk basins, bubbling up from the earth. When I was a boy they were a familiar enough phenomenon in my native downland village of Pitton. And, as in Tilshead, they used to ooze up in the village street or under householders' floor-boards or in other inconvenient places. One well-known spring used to burst through a living-room hearth. Villagers watched the water level in wells and would predict sagaciously, 'Ah, the springs'll be down next wik.' I have the pocket-books of an old villager who, while using most of the pages for records of his garden vegetables and the hurdles he made and sold, noted down on the inside covers some of the most outstanding events of his lifetime. He remembered, more than thirty years later, the text of the sermon preached at the reopening of the church after restoration in the 1880s. But the most important happenings within his narrow horizons seem to have been the occurrence of 'the springs', of which he kept a complete record. Although irregular in their appearance, they seem to have broken through, on average, about once every seven years, forming considerable lakes, linked by a flowing stream, all along the valley. One of the lakes was in the middle of the village, and old people remember that, back in the 1850s or thereabouts, a fever epidemic occurred in April and May, due, it was said, to the pools of stagnant water lying about when the spring receded. So the villagers set to work to dig a channel whereby, in the future, the water could escape. The channel was kept reasonably clear till the time of the second world war, since when it has been encroached on by roads and buildings. Old-timers have shaken their heads and uttered prophecies of doom when next the springs break, but so far their forecasts have been unrealised, so far below its former levels has the water table sunk. The last time Pitton was partly under water was at some time between 1955 and 1960. Still, more recent experiences of Tilshead and other chalkland villages shows that the danger is not entirely past. Maybe next winter or the one after the village children will enjoy the fun that all the youngsters of my generation enjoyed – of boating on 'the springs' in a variety of home-made and ramshackle craft, prominent among which, in my recollection, was a barn door, punted along by a clothes'-prop. Not many of us escaped a ducking.

Two Almost Forgotten Festivals

A reader drew my attention to an almost forgotten date in the rural calendar. April 23rd, he said, is the traditional date for making dandelion wine. The brew made on any other day is never as good.

He added that it used to be said that all the best home-brewed beer or ale was made on Sunday mornings! When explained, the reason for this is logical. It relates to the days when men worked for six days a week. After work on Saturdays they would collect the yeast from the baker in readiness for brewing the next morning. If kept longer than that the yeast 'went off'.

Which reminds me that May 22nd to the 24th are, in the Devon calendar, the Feast of St. Frankin, or Frankanmass. St. Frankin, according to local tradition, was a brewer at a time when the brewing trade was being seriously affected by the competition provided by cider. So Frankin sold his soul to the Devil in return for a promise of hard frosts in the period May 22nd–24th to ruin the cider-apple crop! The Devil hasn't fulfilled his part of the bargain this year. The apple prospects have never looked better.

May Day

'May Day's breaking;
All the world's awaking;
Come and see the sun rise
Over the Plain.

'Why have you awoke me?
How you do provoke me!
Let me have a little time
To doze off again.

'Sleeping in the day-time,
Waste the happy Maytime,
Makes an empty pocket and
A cloudy brain.'

That round, which I learned to sing when a small boy at primary school, was about the only reference to May Day I ever heard in our Wiltshire village. Mention of the Plain, which I presume means Salisbury Plain, makes me think it is of local origin, but from the style I imagine it is not all that old. No, in our village, as in so any others in the West Country, the significance of May Day, once a major red letter day in the calendar, has been almost entirely forgotten.

However, some of the old customs survived until just before my time. In 1896 a visitor to Wiltshire met little girls parading the streets with garlands in Salisbury and Wilton. They had woven flowers around short sticks, which they showed to passers-by, who were expected to put something in the collecting bag. The Wilton garland-bearers sang a little song, concluding with the line 'Please give a penny for the garland'. The Salisbury children apparently did not sing but their garlands were said to have been more elaborate.

Making garlands was one of the recognised activities of May Day, and in some districts the children devoted the whole of April 30th to it. Now I come to think of it, when in the infant's class at school we were sent out to gather cowslips and shown how to make them into 'cowslip-balls'; perhaps that was connected with May Day. In other parts of the country children paraded with dolls, dressed in finery and framed in garlanded hoops. The dolls were covered with a cloth, which was removed to display the doll to any passer-by who asked to see it and was prepared to pay for the privilege.

These customs were the last pale survivals of the formerly full-blooded May festivities, appropriately known as 'revels'. In bygone days every village elected its May Queen, and sometimes a May King as well. Sometimes she was identified as Maid Marian, the consort of Robin Hood, doubtless because of May Day associations with the greenwood. Another prominent character was the Chimney Sweep, or Jack-in-the-Green. At Amesbury people were alive in the 1930s who could remember the May Day Feast and recollected that it was also known as 'The Sweeps' Holiday', because 'the May Queen danced with the Chimney Sweep'. So it was apparently at St. Marybourne, in Hampshire, where the local sweeps assembled to dance around a figure, dressed entirely in green boughs and leaves, called Jack o' the Green.

Morris dancers were out in strength on May Day, leading the processions. And many places possessed a Hobby Horse, which pranced around, snapping at the spectators and demanding alms. Minehead, on the Exmoor coast, has two Hobby Horses, which still appear regularly on May Day. Salisbury too has a Hobby Horse, though there are no longer May Day processions for it to appear in. The focus of the May Day festivities was usually the Maypole, around which the parishioners danced. In some districts it was a custom for the young men of one parish to raid their neighbours and endeavour to steal their Maypole. At Cerne Abbas the Maypole used to be erected in the earthwork on the hill just above the head of the Giant.

Yet another feature of the May Day festivities was the practice of the young men and girls to spend the previous night in the woods. The whole basis of the May Day celebrations was originally a pagan fertility ritual, and the Puritans recognised them as such and strenuously opposed them. The merry-making came to an end during the period of the Commonwealth, and

when it was resumed on the restoration of Charles II it became diffused. A great many May Day customs got transferred to May 29th, Oak Apple Day, the date of the restoration of the monarchy. Typical are the Oak Apple Day junketings at Wishford, Wiltshire, where the parishioners, aroused by a terrific hullabaloo at about 2.30a.m., trudge the mile or so up the downland path to Groveley Wood to cut green boughs. These they drag down to the village to decorate the houses, one of the largest branches being hauled to the top of the church tower. Prizes are offered for the spray of oak bearing most oak apples. The event is said to commemorate a successful campaign to thwart the efforts of a local landowner to prevent the villagers from exercising their ancient right to cut green boughs in Groveley on that morning, and so it may, but it has a much earlier origin. It is, in fact, typical of what went on in innumerable villages in mediaeval England. Another West Country village which preserves memories of an almost identical custom is Whitchurch Canonicorum, in Dorset.

Another disrupting influence was the change in the calendar in the year 1752, when eleven days were 'lost'. In the 1920s Miss Edith Olivier found old people still living who could remember when May Day was kept up in traditional style at Durrington, on Salisbury Plain. 'The men went to the downs and got a may-bush and then to the Nag's Head Inn for the maypole. They tied the bush to the top of the May-pole and chained the pole to the top of the Cross Stones. All this happened the night before, when it was dark. In the evening of Old May Day they danced around the Cross Stones to the music of concertina and whistle-pipes. They also had cakes and barrels of beer to eat and drink.' An interesting detail was that this celebration took place on Old May Day – May 13th – and not the present May 1st.

It is unlucky to bring marsh marigolds into the house on May Day. Dew, gathered and applied before daybreak, was supposed to be good for the complexion; it would even obliterate freckles. Collected from a churchyard, it is used to be considered a cure for consumption. Runner beans should be planted on or about May Day, and, in any case, by May 6th. Hawthorn twigs stuck in the seed-bed help to protect the young plants against the malice of witches!

'May kittens never make good cats' is an old and widespread belief, which never made sense to me. I would have thought May was about the very best month for any animal to be born.

Midsummer

June 30th, 1978

Midsummer has crept up on me unawares. Not that it is surprising, for the calendar in the last half of June is decidedly confusing. If March 21st is the first day of spring, June 21st must be the first day of summer; and Midsummer Day is June 24th, so that gives us just seven or eight days of summer – which cynics will say is about what we usually get! To add to the confusion, the longest day is June 22nd, though I believe that originally it coincided with Midsummer Day.

In the church calendar Midsummer Day is the Feast of St. John the Baptist, held to be appropriate because of the saying of John, as recorded in the Gospels, who, referring to Christ, said, 'He must increase, but I must decrease'. On Midsummer Day the sun, like John the Baptist on that occasion, is at its zenith; thereafter it begins to decline. St. John's-wort is so called because it is in flower on St. John the Baptist's Day, but it has an older association with Midsummer because its golden colour was thought to indicate its dedication to the sun. An old-time country custom was to hang bunches of St. John's-wort around the doors and windows of houses at Midsummer, to ward off witches and evil spirits.

There was a very ancient belief that on Midsummer Eve the spirits of the living leave their mortal bodies and wander freely. In particular they visit the spot where, in due course, they will quit their body permanently. It follows that they are interested in churches and graveyards.

So the tradition arose that anyone who had the temerity to sit in the church porch all through the night of Midsummer Eve would see pass before him, in procession, all those souls in the parish who would die within the next year, parading in order of decease. Some versions said you had to hide in the churchyard in a spot where you could see the church porch. A pragmatic approach to the matter was displayed by a Yorkshire sexton who, it is said, regularly kept vigil on Midsummer Eve in order to calculate his income from grave-digging in the coming year!

Obviously one's spirit could leave the body only if one were asleep, which was a good reason for keeping awake all through the witching hours of Midsummer Eve. If a watcher keeping vigil at a church himself fell asleep, that was a sure sign that he would be one of the fatalities in the coming year. Probably from this belief arose the custom of Midsummer Wakes. Even at Midsummer it can be chilly in the small hours, so we can understand that watchers, afraid to go to sleep, would prefer to move around. Centuries ago people engaged in 'marching watches', parading around town or village with torches and garlands. Householders would set tables outside their doors and serve refreshments to neighbours and passers-by.

Spirits are, of course, invisible, but there would be decided advantages in being bodily invisible too. This could be achieved, according to old-time tradition, by shaking fern leaves at midnight on Midsummer Eve so that their 'seeds' (spores) fell into pewter plates held beneath them. Possession of these spores (themselves almost invisible) enabled a man to wander at will in the Otherworld. On a more practical level, he might also spy on his lady love, which made the practice popular with young men. However, the gatherers of fern seed had to be cautious and lucky, for the Devil resented human beings acquiring such supernatural powers and did his best to prevent it.

Unmarried girls also used fern seed to learn the identity of their future husbands. The seed had to be scattered at midnight on Midsummer Eve while the girl recited:

'Fern seed I sow;
Fern seed I hoe;
In hopes my true love will come after me and mow.'

This she did as she ran three times around the church while the clock was striking midnight. On the third course she could glance over her shoulder and see the ghost of her future husband following her and mowing with a scythe.

Some versions of the rhyme substitute 'hemp seed' for 'fern seed'. As hemp seed is better known today as cannabis, one is inclined to wonder just what part it played in such old-time practices.

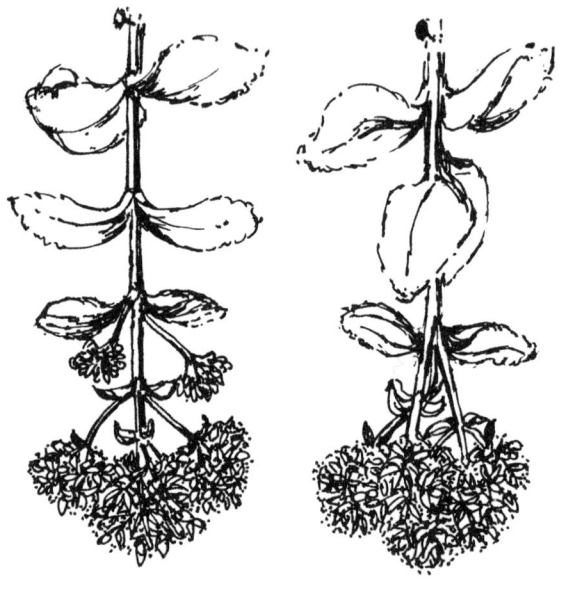

Divination was much in fashion at Midsummer. One method employed by girls eager to know whether their lovers would be true to them was to hang two stems of orpine, a fleshy-leaved flower which blooms at this season, side by side in their room at night. If they bent towards each other, all would be well; if they turned away from each other, the girl would be jilted. Orpine lasts for weeks after picking, either in or out of water, which, I suppose, made it seem suitable as a symbol of undying love. The plant was also known as Livelong; also as Midsummer Men.

Another plant valued for divination was mugwort, an unattractive weed of the dock family. It was said that under some mugwort roots could be found a piece of coal, which had magical properties. This coal had to be dug up on Midsummer Eve at midnight (or, according to another version, at mid-day) and placed under the pillow when the girl retired to rest. She would then dream of her future husband. The 'coal' is actually a decayed part of the root.

A procedure not connected with plants but undertaken for the same purpose was for a girl, on Midsummer Eve, to turn a clean chemise inside out, damp it and hang it over the back of a chair before the fire, all in complete silence. The girl's future husband would then enter the house and turn the chemise. It would seem a most improbable sequence of events, unless pre-arrangements had been made.

A common feature of Midsummer festivities in the old days was the Midsummer Bonfire. You danced around the Bonfire clockwise, in imitation of the sun following his course across the heavens. Blazing brands were taken from the fire and carried around house and cattle stall, also clockwise, to protect the inmates from illness (or witches, which was the same thing, for witches were held to be responsible for sickness). In some places people leaped through the bonfire or drove their cattle through, as the flames began to die down, with the same object in mind.

An attractive superstition was that a rose plucked at Midsummer would keep fresh until Christmas. The girl who picked it had then to wear it to church, when her future husband would come and take it from her.

All these traditions belong to a long time back, most of them well beyond living memory, but it would be interesting to know if any readers have other recollections of customs or sayings connected with Midsummer. About the only one I can think of is an alleged Devonshire proverb, 'Before St. John's Day we pray for rain; afterwards we get it anyhow!'

A Sherborne reader told me that when a girl in Cumberland she heard that, if on Midsummer Eve you walked three times around a rose-tree at midnight and wished, you would marry the one you loved. She remembers staying awake till midnight on the magic date and then stealing across the lawn in her nightdress (in that high northern latitude it was still only twilight) to where a large rose tree was covered with white blossom. After walking round it three times, murmuring the name of her hero of the moment, she plucked a petal from one of the roses and slept with it under her pillow.

The spell didn't work. She assured me that eventually she married very happily, but not to that man!

Lammas Tide

The first week-end of August is the date of an old country festival now largely forgotten – Lammas tide. In the pre-Christian Celtic calendar it was a quarter day, marking the beginning of harvest. Christianised, it became the Festival of the First-fruits. It is still a full quarter day in Scotland. From the first wheat harvested after Lammas tide (August 1st) bread for use in the sacrament of Holy Communion was traditionally made, and in recent years the custom has been revived in some places, communicants being offered locally-made 'Lammas bread'. In remote parts of Devon farmers not so long ago used to take four pieces of Lammas bread and crumble them in the four quarters of their barn, presumably either as a votive offering or to give the building and its contents some protection against evil.

Many West Country fairs were traditionally held at Lammas tide and were known as Lammas Fairs. Perhaps the best known is the surviving Lammas Fair at Exeter, and Wiltshire had several fairs which were slightly removed in the calendar from August 1st but were almost certainly once associated with Lammas. One was Tan Hill Fair, held on Tan Hill, near All Cannings, on August 6th; another was at Cricklade on the first Sunday after August 12th. The great sheep fair at Britford, near Salisbury, on August 12th was also probably a Lammas Fair, for the Celtic Lammas, or Lugnasad, belonged to a pastoral calendar organised to fit in with the needs of keepers of flocks and herds. Lammas Fairs were very convenient occasions for selling off the season's crop of lambs.

Lammas was also the date when lands that had been laid up for haymaking reverted to common grazing. In Wiltshire it used to be the custom for the water-meadows in the chalk valleys to be grazed by sheep in spring, then fenced off for the grass to grow for haymaking, and then, when the hay was safely made, opened for grazing again, about Lammas tide. The Cricklade Lammas Fair was associated with the right of every commoner of the parish to turn out nine cattle to graze on the 114-acre Cricklade Common from Lammas to Candlemas.

The Lammas Fairs used to feature many boisterous old-time sports. At Cricklade, for instance, the programme used to include 'bull-baiting, hack-swording, boxing, wrestling, cock-fighting, "breakheads" (played with cudgels) and "kick-legs".' Something very similar, though even less inhibited, used evidently to go on in the Celtic districts of Britain. Once on a visit to the Isle of Man I heard of the old custom of climbing to the top of Snaefell, the highest peak on the island, on the first Sunday in August and there engaging in behaviour which was described as being 'very rude and indecent'. The Church protested frequently but vainly against the scandalous goings-on until one Lammas tide a chapel preacher solved the problem by holding a service on the hill-top and passing around the collecting plate! The crowd just melted away!

Although the most favoured theory is that the word 'Lammas' is derived from 'Loaf-mass', the festival of loaves, an alternative one is that it is really 'Lamb-mass' and refers to the lambs brought to the church as tithes on St. Peter's Day. This would tie in with the association of Lammas tide with sheep rather than with cultivated crops.

BIRDS AND BEASTS

Gabbygammies and Edible Dormice

The village of Ashmore, on the Dorset hills, used to have a family of ghosts. They haunted a barrow on the downs not far from the village and were known as the *Gabbygammies* or *Gappergennies*. No-one ever saw them but they could be heard prowling around at nights, making a variety of strange noises. Understandably, no-one ever went near the tumulus to investigate. Modern opinion, however, divorced as usual from all romance, suggests that the barrow was the home of a family of badgers.

I thought of the Gabbygammies when I received a letter from a Sandford Orcas reader who is also haunted by what in times past would have been inevitably identified as a family of ghosts. He writes:–

'We reside in an old thatched house, recently re-thatched and wired on top. A year ago we suffered considerable disturbance at nights from the loft above our bedroom. At the same time I noticed a pair of grey squirrels in the garden and by watching them discovered that they had found a way into the roof. They were subsequently shot, and work done on the house last summer effectively blocked all entrances to the roof.

However, a few weeks ago we had another visitor. We feel sure it is not a squirrel, for none has been seen in the neighbourhood. Whatever it is is silent during the day but moves around at night. It appears to have a nest or perhaps two under the thatch. We have not been able to find any droppings; we have prodded the roof with bamboos; we have liberally scattered mouse and rat poison; we have set traps baited with cheese, chocolate and nuts; we have poured out ammonia and scattered pepper. All to no avail.

Have you any suggestions as to what it is and how to get rid of it? Incidentally, the creature does not utter any sounds; it just pulls out straw and rolls pieces of wood about! Is it a glis-glis?'

Yes, without much doubt it is. A glis-glis is another name for the fat or edible dormouse, some specimens of which were introduced into Hertfordshire by Lord Rothschild in about 1890. Since then it has become well established and has extended its range over several Midland counties, though I have not previously heard of any so far west. I had some experience of these dormice on the Chilterns in Buckinghamshire six or seven years ago, and they behaved exactly as my correspondent describes. There a colony had become established in the roof of a forester's cottage and had defied attempts to persuade them to leave.

The edible dormouse is much bigger than our English dormouse, reaching a length of six or seven inches, with a further six inches of tail. Indeed, it looks more like a miniature grey squirrel than a dormouse, for its tail is bushy, or rather fuzzy, and its colour is grey rather than golden. It has very large, bright eyes. In autumn it fattens up on nuts, berries, fruit and insects, storing the surplus it collects. Then it hibernates, but wakes up from time to time for a feed. The Romans used to fatten it as a delicacy for rich men's banquets, and I think that perhaps it is still so treated in parts of Europe.

Attics and roofs are its favourite home, especially in wooded country, and it is always nocturnal. So the behaviour described at Sandford Orcas is typical.

I have suggested to my correspondent that he does nothing further about his guests but learns to live with them. After a time he may grow to enjoy listening to their nocturnal activities. To have such a colony in one's house is probably unique in the West Country, and a good story could be hatched about resident ghosts. Anyhow, I doubt whether there is much choice in the matter, for edible dormice are persistent little creatures. When they come, they come to stay.

The Hornéd Hare

At Winterslow, near Salisbury, Lyddie Shears, a witch who lived there some time in the late eighteenth or early nineteenth centuries, was a valued collaborator of local poachers in taking hares. She would turn herself into a hare and help to drive other hares into the poachers' nets. So flagrant did her activities become that a resident landowner swore to eliminate the menace.

Loading his muzzle-loading gun with a silver bullet (traditionally effective against witches) he found her one night in the guise of a large hare, rounding up a pack of them. He scored a direct hit, and the hare limped away, dripping blood. The trail led to her cottage, and there Lyddie Shears was found dead, a silver bullet in her heart.

So reads one of Wiltshire's favourite witchcraft stories. Hares were notorious witch animals, and it is no wonder that legends and tales about them abound. Indeed, so curious is some of the behaviour of this enigmatic animal that it is difficult to disentangle fact from fiction.

The yarn that there is a race of hornéd hares was once widely believed. It was proved to the satisfaction of numerous eminent men by the apparently incontrovertible evidence of stuffed hares with horns attached. Oliver Goldsmith, for instance, declared that not only were there hares that 'are entirely black but even some have been found with horns, though these but rarely'. Henry Tegner in his excellent book *Wild Hares* claims to have seen stuffed specimens in which the tiny horns of young roebuck have been cunningly inserted in the head of a hare. The fraud could perhaps be classified as giving the customer what he wanted.

Is the hare a ruminant animal? No, of course not; and yet folk lore insists that it chews the cud. Even the Book of Leviticus classifies it as unclean for that reason. And, in a way, there is some justification for the view. An animal which chews the cud regurgitates its food and gives it a second mastication several hours after first swallowing it. The hare allows the undigested food to pass through it and then eats its own pellets. So the two processes are approximately parallel, though the habit is so repulsive to human beings that many races in antiquity, including the Celts in Britain (from whom much of our hare lore is derived), regarded it as unclean.

Baby hares, as is well known, are born with a full coat of fur and with their eyes open, unlike rabbits, which go through a period of blind helplessness. The leverets occupy forms in the open fields, where they squat motionless. But what is controversial is whether the mother hare gives birth to her babies in different places or whether, after they are born, she picks them up and carries them to dispersed places of concealment. Old countrymen incline to the view that she carries them, grasping them by the scruff of the neck, as a cat does kittens, but I have never met anyone who has actually seen the operation.

Doe hares usually have two leverets at a birth, but occasionally there are three. Country tradition says that when this occurs, the third leveret has a white star on its forehead.

Hares moult twice a year, but they retain their summer coat for only a month or two. The first moult, to get rid of their winter coat, occurs anywhere between February and June; the second, in readiness for growing the next winter coat, at some time between July and October.

Does a hare drink? There is a general idea that it does not, but people who have kept tame hares testify that it does. Hares are quite easily tamed when taken young. Many countrymen, as boys, have picked up baby hares from their forms and fed them with warm milk from old-fashioned fountain-pen fillers. A lady I know who had three hares fed them with a mixture of oats, glucose, milk and a proprietary cereal, taken from a spoon. She told me that they were easily house-trained and that they quickly developed strong individual characteristics.

Of her three hares, two were young and one adult. When the older hare had had enough of romping with the couple of wild juniors she stamped her back feet; the young hares then immediately became motionless and did not move for some time. Other householders who have acted as hosts to pet hares have remarked on the enjoyment the hares found in drumming with their fore-paws on boxes or other hollow containers that would give a good, resonant sound. Stamping on the ground is the wild hare's natural means of communication with others of its kind, and it could even have a code or rudimentary language. No doubt its huge ears are very sensitive to vibrations, which accounts for the old belief that a hare can hear thunder long before it is audible to human ears.

It has also been suggested that hares like the noise of aircraft. Certainly they tend to congregate on airfields, as can be confirmed by anyone who ever landed at Nutts Corner airfield, near Belfast. But it is curious that when the planes moved to a new landing-ground four miles away, the hares, of which huge packs swarmed over Nutts Corner, moved there too.

Open spaces are, of course, attractive to hares because they allow the animals to see the approach of danger from any direction. Country folk believe that a hare runs in circles, and it will indeed, when disturbed, make a long detour and finish up approximately where it started. It dislikes running downhill, when its long hind legs are at a disadvantage, and it prefers to follow contours. Even when being chased, the hare is a cautious animal. It will never take a waterfilled ditch or small brook in a running leap but will pause at the edge and then spring over.

A section on *Hunting* in an old rural encyclopedia, dated 1806, reveals more knowledge of the behaviour of a hunted hare than most countrymen now possess.

'Some hares have been so crafty that, as soon as they have heard the sound of a horn, they would instantly start out of their form, though it was at the distance of a quarter of a mile, and go and swim in some pool, and rest upon some rush-bed in the midst of it; and would not stir from thence till they have heard the sound of the horn again, and then have started out again, swimming to land ... Nay, such is the natural craft and subtlety of a hare that sometimes after she has been hunted for three hours she will start a fresh hare and squat in the same form. Others, having been hunted for a considerable time, will creep under the door of a sheep-cot and hide themselves among the sheep; or when they have been hard hunted, will run in among a flock of sheep and will by no means be gotten out from among them until the hounds are coupled up or the sheep driven into their pens. Some of them (and that seems somewhat strange) will take the ground like a coney, and that is called "going to the vault". Some hares will go up one side of the hedge and come down the other, the thickness of the hedge being the only distance between the courses. A hare that has been hard hunted has got upon a quickset hedge and run a good distance on the top thereof and then leapt off upon the ground. And they will frequently betake themselves to furze bushes and will leap from one to the other, whereby the hounds are frequently at fault ...'

A Dorset villager told me, 'My experience is that hares almost invariably run in circles when hunted, – in order to return to familiar territory, I presume. I can, however, remember one three-mile run in a straight line. I have also known a hunted hare to double back and run right through the beagle pack. When possible a hare runs uphill because of its long legs. But I can remember an occasion when the beagles followed a hare up the north slope of the downs, only to bring us down again immediately. By the time our feet, stumbling downhill, had touched the level ground the hare had scampered to the top of the downs again ...'

After myxomatosis, in 1953 to 1955, hares tended to increase, through absence of competition from rabbits, but the population seems to have levelled off now.

I go Hawking

(The following account of an afternoon's hawking appeared in the *Western Gazette*, in my Countryside column, on February 10th, 1950).

'The hawk we used was a Goshawk, brought down from London by the falconer. He travelled in an ordinary third-class compartment, with the hawk sitting on his wrist. The hawk perched quietly, fastened to his leather gauntlet and watching with her bright orange-and-brown eyes her somewhat apprehensive fellow-passengers.

A Goshawk is a giant edition of the Sparrow-hawk. This one, being a female (for females are larger than males), is about twice the size of the average Sparrow-hawk but very similar in colour. She weighs two pounds, five ounces. Goshawks are fast over a short course but can seldom capture game on the wing. Their chief prey is rabbits, though they will also pick up moorhens, coot and other birds which run, and they are not to be trusted with poultry. We went rabbiting with ours.

The first two rabbits we let her fly at escaped into hedges. The third, beaten from a field of kale, chose to run across open ground, and the hawk, in an almost leisurely manner, dived on it before it had travelled thirty yards. She sank her talons into the rabbit's back and held it on the ground until her master came up. Then she allowed him to take it from her. She perched on his glove again and was rewarded with a titbit of raw rabbit flesh.

At this juncture a storm blew up and called a halt to the afternoon's activities. High wind is fatal to hawking. If the hawk misses her stoop she often sweeps into the air to reconnoitre for a second try, and a strong wind will sometimes carry her for a mile or more before she recovers her poise. That is how hawks get lost.

The falconer estimates that our afternoon's results were about average. We had one rabbit from three stoops, and he estimates that, in hawking with a Goshawk, the rabbit's chance of escape is about 60% or 70%.

This Goshawk came from Norway. Occasionally a wild bird occurs in Britain, usually as a wanderer to the eastern counties, though centuries ago it may have been a regular nester.

An Egg-Hunting Cat

I was told an interesting story of a cat who collected birds' eggs. This cat, a ginger neuter, appeared crossing the lawn by the house with something white protruding from his mouth. The garden door being shut, he somehow climbed a seven-foot wall and was then seen jumping down five feet from it on the other side on to a small roof, from which he made his usual entry into the house by the dining-room window. Once there, he laid the still intact white object on the carpet, for the admiration of the assembled family circle, ... and they saw – a wood-pigeon's egg! Earlier in the day a similar unbroken egg had been found on the path just by the roof mentioned, and there seems no doubt that it too had been brought there by the cat.

Queenie Loves People

I met Queenie, at a farming event at Curry Rivel, Somerset, on September 2nd and 3rd, 1978, strolling placidly around with a small boy on her back. At a word of command she sat down gracefully and remained contentedly chewing her cud, while children played around and fondled her and canned music blared a few yards away.

Anyone who attended Yeovil Carnival in the previous autumn had seen Queenie before. She was then a seven-weeks-old calf who sat docilely on the Yesterday's Farming float as it was towed around the streets. Queenie loves crowds; she loves people, and she loves music.

Her owner, Mr. Don Vickery, of Highway Farm, Ash, near Martock, spotted this when she was only a few weeks old. Being convinced, like many other farmers, that cows like music, he had coupled his milking machine with a radio set so that when the machine is switched on the BBC Radio 1 programme comes on automatically. All the cows seem to like it, and other farmers have told me they consider that they let down their milk more easily, but Queenie at a very early age showed signs of especially enjoying it. She also loved children to come and play with her, trying to follow them when they left.

So Don Vickery, recognising that he had a somewhat unusual animal on his hands, gave her every opportunity to develop her personality. All through her adolescence she lived in an orchard of her own and saw more of humans than she did of other cattle. She sought human company as much as possible and was never happier than when she had children to visit and play with her, allowing them to ride her and romp over her to their hearts' content.

She enjoyed another year of her eccentric career, after which she was mated in preparation for settling down to life in the herd. 'She will change a bit then,' said Mr. Vickery, but, in fact, she has continued to be as docile as ever and to enjoy music. Incidentally, she seems to show no particular preference for any sort of music. Some other farmers whom I have heard relaying music to their milking-parlours have considered that the cows should have soothing or classical music, but BBC 1 transmits quite a lot of 'pop' music, I believe. It seems to be all one to Queenie; it's the noise she likes.

Although Queenie is a decidedly unusual animal, farmers who have set out to train cattle, bulls in particular, for riding tell me they experience little difficulty. Some have trained a succession of bovine steeds over a period of years. Some of the animals show a certain aptitude in their early days, but it is more a matter of taking an obviously quiet animal while it is young and getting it accustomed to being handled.

Much the same applies to most domestic livestock. We expect dogs, and to a certain extent cats, to develop a personality, much of it derived from their owners, but tend to regard such development in other animals as somewhat freakish. Most of them would respond, however, if given an equal opportunity. Pigs are among the most intelligent of animals, quite equal to a dog. As a boy on a farm, I remember having individuals of most types of farm animals as pets at one time or another. I remember a goose, for instance, a duck, a goat or two, a pet lamb, one or two highly individual hens, ponies and, of course, rabbits and guinea pigs. Even the duck, named Octo (because she was the only survivor of a brood of eight), became quite a character, quacking loudly for us to take her into the garden at certain times of the day and lift up rockery stones for her to gobble the snails clustering underneath them. I think that perhaps personality is a gift that we can bestow on members of the animal kingdom.

That was easier forty years ago than it is now. When a farmer had a dozen cows he had more opportunity to study the character of each one than he has now, with a herd of a hundred or two. Many a cottager in the old days, chased out of the house on a Sunday morning by his wife, would spend a contented hour or two communing with the pig in the sty at the end of the garden. Such an exercise would be impossible in a modern piggery. As for poultry, how can one even notice an individual in a batch of ten thousand? Apart from which, most chicken now die long before they reach maturity.

The human species is about the only one to which modern principles of selective breeding have not been applied. We breed dairy cattle for the efficient production of milk (far in excess of what would be normally needed for a calf), beef cattle for producing meat, pigs for producing bacon (and the more uniformity we can achieve the better we are pleased), table chicken for quick maturity, laying hens for the efficient production of eggs, and so on. I wonder what would happen if we took a heifer like Queenie and started to breed cattle for intelligence? By mating an intelligent bull with an intelligent cow and selecting the most intelligent offspring for a few generations it might well be possible to lay the foundations of a super-race of cattle.

Perhaps cattle would not be the ideal species. Pigs would be more promising, having a pretty high level of intelligence to start with. It is, of course, unlikely to happen, for there would be no profit in it, as far as one can see. Indeed, the reverse could possibly be true. And what if the end of the experiment were the same as the climax of George Orwell's *Animal Farm*? The other animals, it will be remembered, looked through the window to where the pigs and the humans were quarrelling, and, looking from one to the other, they had a job to tell the difference between them.

A Fish-eating Blackbird

In December, 1976 a Verwood reader, harking back to the summer drought, told me that she rescued quite a lot of minnows from tiny pools left among the pebbles when some of the New Forest streams dried up. As it was only a matter of days before those last pools would dry up too, she took the little fish home and kept them in bowls and buckets.

'One day a blackbird flew over a bowl of fish, swooped and flew off with one in his beak. I quickly put an old piece of net curtain over the bowl, and it was just as well that I did, for back the bird came and started to pull at the material with his beak.'

She added that this was a cock blackbird who at the time was helping to feed a brood of young, but, even so, for a blackbird to eat fish seems extraordinary. I have consulted *The Handbook of British Birds* and see that it gives only one instance of a blackbird bringing a stranded minnow to a nest.

A Cannibal Fox?

A Mere reader asked my opinion about a fox incident she witnessed on an early morning in May.

'Fox emerged from a hedgerow and, on seeing me, dropped what I thought was a rabbit and disappeared through the hedge on the opposite side of the road. It had been carrying the head and fore-legs of a freshly-killed young cub. I waited further up the road, but the fox did not retrieve it.'

I can think of three alternative explanations.

1. That the fox was a vixen tenderly carrying the body of one of her cubs that had been killed, perhaps by a car. This is the sentimental explanation.

2. That the fox was a dog fox who had likewise discovered the dead cub and was taking it away to eat it.

3. That the fox was a dog fox who had found and killed the cub and, having half eaten it, was going to bury the other half for future use.

The second two are the likeliest. Dog foxes, like tom cats, can be cannibals and are not to be trusted with their own offspring.

The Dance of the Adders

From Semley, in South-west Wiltshire, I received, in May, 1978 the following account.

'At 10.45 a.m. on May 8th, I was sitting on a portable stool at the top of Tittlepath Hill, above Semley, watching a pair of tree pipits which I was convinced were about to nest in the vicinity. The weather was dull and cool. My attention was caught by what at first appeared to be a strand of bramble, five or ten yards away, moving in the light wind.

'Almost instantly came the realization that it was not a bramble but a rather dark-coloured adder. And I saw that the rear half of the body was coiled around part of a second lighter-coloured adder, making what could be described as a loose knot.

'The two snakes continued to writhe about and gradually assumed a vertical position, their heads being about level with the remaining stems of dead bracken, about a foot above the ground. This posture they maintained for two or three minutes, remaining in the same place although their bodies were never still. Finally the lighter specimen subsided from view into the dead vegetation, while the other remained extended over the dead bracken fronds.

'I had heard of this ritual or ceremony among adders and have spoken to one other person who has seen it – in Great Ridge Wood a year or two ago. We are thinking of forming a club, with an appropriate tie!'

And I, unfortunately, would not be able to join the club, for I have never seen this 'dance of the adders'. One needs to be in the right place at the right time (late April or early May, when the adders are ready to mate), and then to have a lot of luck.

The 'dance' used to be considered a mating ceremony, with a male and female snake involved, but then it was realized that in every instance both the adders were males. It is now appreciated that it is a kind of trial of strength by two rival males, on a par with the behaviour of animals and birds in the mating season. The two snakes at Semley were probably being watched not only by a fascinated human being but also by a female adder, curled up in the bracken nearby. There may have been others, too, for adders tend to congregate in small groups at this time of the year.

It must require a considerable amount of muscular strength on the part of the snakes to hold themselves erect for several minutes while writhing about and trying to force their rival to capitulate. As is usual in nature, the strongest wins and so takes the female. The ritual always follows the same pattern, and there is no biting.

This story prompted several readers to write to say they too had seen the 'dance of the adders'. A Morden (Wareham) correspondent sent me two stories of adders on the Dorset heaths, where they are quite common.

Fifteen or so years ago he saw two adders going through the motions of what he then thought was mating. Unfortunately just as he was getting interested his small daughter attracted his attention to the fact that she too was watching ... from a hillock crawling with red ants! Her yells scared the adders away.

A year or two later his son, in his absence, found a particularly large adder and managed to coax it into a large sweet jar, after which he ran a mile to telephone the Nature Conservancy warden. This experienced naturalist, having transferred the snake to a specially-prepared tin, remarked that where one was found there were often two, and, sure enough, he found the second.

One was killed, for examination, but the big one which was the first capture was put in a snake compound that the warden had established.

'Our champion was a fighter,' says my informant, 'and off he went in search of the local gentry. Soon he found the local bigwig and, getting his head underneath, tossed him high in the air.' It was, the naturalist assured him, a straightforward battle for superiority in a confined space, but evidently on this occasion the newcomer had no time for such formal rituals as 'the dance of the adders'.

In winter about the same time, when a wall was being repaired at Handford School, near Blandford, a ball of snakes was found, curled up together. Unfortunately the ball was split up by workmen before it could be expertly examined, but my informant thinks that it was composed of nearly all either grass-snakes or slow-worms, with only one adder. In so doing he has illustrated one of the more puzzling problems that still confront naturalists. One would hardly expect to find adders curled up with lizards (which slow-worms are) or grass-snakes, seeing that they often prey on both these species, but people who have unearthed these hibernating clusters usually say that the composition was mixed. Unfortunately, such balls are generally discovered by accident and are usually dispersed before they are properly examined.

Why are Animal Tracks not straight?

Animals, both wild and domestic, prefer to follow well-trodden paths – a fact which has been exploited to bring about the downfall of innumerable rabbits, hares, deer, rats and other animals from time immemorial. If cows or sheep are turned regularly into a field, they soon wear a path across it. But have you ever seen a *straight* path made by animals? And have you ever wondered why not?

Thinking about this, and examining the tracks of cattle, sheep, rabbits and rats, I have formed a theory which will bear further investigation. It is that when an animal starts to cross an open field it bears instinctively to the left. Human beings do the same. Doubtless we have read of wanderers lost in the wild who have walked in a circle, finishing up where they started. Almost always they veer instinctively to the left ... at least, in the northern hemisphere. I think that south of the equator it is the reverse. The phenomenon has something to do with the spinning of the earth and is paralleled by the behaviour of runner beans, which twine around their poles always in one direction in the northern hemisphere and in the opposite direction in the southern.

Anyway, here are these cows, or rabbits, or whatever, entering a field or a moor and purposing to cross to the other side. After an initial swerve to the left they look ahead and realise that they are going off-course. So they correct their movement. Before long, however, instinct takes over again, and they edge leftwards. So their passage across the field is a series of curves, like the course of a river.

Of course, in certain circumstances other factors are important. On a hillside, for instance, animals tend to follow the contours. Most hillsides where sheep run are patterned in a series of steps, formed by the sheep treading contour paths. Hares, too, tend to run in an enormous circle, finishing up at their starting-point after a course of several miles. They do so, it is said, because of the position of their eyes, which, set prominently in the sides of their heads, enable them to see the countryside on either side better than that straight ahead. But it would be interesting to know whether, in making their large circle, they veer to right or left.

I have been watching gulls in thermals, too, and notice that they generally move in a clockwise direction. It would be interesting to know whether this is invariably so. And which way a lark spirals when it is soaring.

Incidentally, ground birds as well as animals tend to follow the same paths and make 'runs'. The moorhens do in the mud by the stream at the bottom of the orchard, and pheasants do in hedgerows. Old countrymen used to claim that larks did. They said that a sky-lark, alighting after soaring, would always do so several yards from its nest and then run in to the nest, forming a path in which a horsehair noose could be set to catch it. But their eyes must have been sharper than mine, for I have never managed to detect such a path.

Two readers took me to task over these notes on why animals make wriggly tracks. They declared that I ought to know better. It is, they said, because the animals follow natural force-waves emanating from the soil – the sort of waves that dowsers find with their rods.

I know the theory. Its chief exponent was Guy Underwood, who died in 1964 and whose book, *The Pattern of the Past*, was reprinted as a paperback in 1974. I can find water by dowsing, but Mr. Underwood must have been far more gifted in that respect than I am, for he found a maze of other phenomena, the chief of which he labelled 'aquastats' and 'track lines'. These force-lines apparently converge on spots which he terms 'blind springs' and form spirals there.

He maintained that animals are sensitive to these force-lines and blind springs. Indeed, some of his claims are astonishing. Cattle and sheep tracks, he says, follow the invisible track-lines. Female animals, from cattle to pigs and dogs, find a blind spring over which to lie to produce their young. Birds also make their nests over blind springs. Cows lie down to sleep on blind springs, and clouds of gnats always choose a blind spring over which to dance. And so on.

Well, he may be right. Far be it from me to assert that anything is impossible. I confess that, though I can locate water, pipelines and certain metals by dowsing, these secondary lines are completely beyond me. There are so many of them. Mr. Underwood plots scores of them around and across single stones at Stonehenge.

But I cannot go along with the theory that cattle and other animal tracks are not straight because the animals instinctively follow the force-lines. Here is a large field, into which a herd of cows goes to graze every day. Beyond is another field, to which they have access. Before long they have made a track across the first field to the gateway into the second. It is never a straight line, for it wobbles from side to side, but it arrives safely at its destination. Mr. Underwood counters this by stating that old field entrances are usually over blind springs, but the behaviour of the cows is exactly the same if they are making for a new entrance, which I have just made for them without reference to blind springs or force-lines. And here is a meadow in which we can trace a whole range of cattle tracks converging on a point somewhere near the centre. Blind spring? No, a water trough!

However, I think we can concede that some animals do have senses that are unfamiliar to us. It is said that a male dog can detect a female on heat two hundred yards or so away even if he is looking at her through glass. In other words, he is doing so by sight, not by smell. If that is so, what does he see?

Commenting on this propensity of animals and plants to move clockwise or anti-clockwise, a Lyme Regis reader wrote:-

'During the nine years in which I kept goats, I noticed that when tethered on their 15-foot chains they always, unless obstructed (say, by their chain becoming entangled on a tuft of grass), walked around the tether in a clockwise direction. I have often wondered whether stud bulls, when tethered in a bull yard, always move in a similar direction.

'Another curious phenomenon. I have noticed lately that if a spoonful of light kaolin powder is poured into a cup of boiling water it invariably rotates in an anti-clockwise direction until it sinks to the bottom of the cup.'

White Cats are Deaf

Are all ginger cats toms and all tortoiseshells females? The answer is that is the general rule but that exceptions do occur. A reader posed the query, 'Are white cats usually deaf?' She had one which was and had been told that the handicap is common.

Yes, it is. It is not an invariable rule, but deafness often occurs in white cats, especially those with pale blue eyes. Whiteness derives from an absence of pigmentation in an animal's make-up and is quite frequently associated with some other deficiency. I remember that when, thirty or forty years ago, my father and I were building up a Dairy Shorthorn herd we bought a white bull and were warned that he would introduce a sterility problem. We thought it was an old wives' tale, but, sure enough, a big proportion of the white heifers he sired were infertile.

A few weeks later a Holcombe (Bath) reader referred to this note. She is on the visiting list of a neighbour's cat who rejoices in the name of Thursday (the cat, not the neighbour) and has one blue eye and one green. It is very affectionate and always hungry, she says, but certainly not deaf or blind. She adds,

'By the look of our clothes and upholstery it is also continually moulting.'

Unlucky Bats

A Bruton reader sent an account of a puzzling occurrence. He writes:

'When reclaiming one of the wilder corners of our far from orderly garden last week I came across a fine specimen of Common Burdock, which I left intact. After sitting close to the plant for some time my wife noticed that what I had taken for a dried leaf was in fact the remains of a bat, which had become stuck on the burdock's spiny flowers and had presumably starved to death. I cut down the offending branch and its victim but left the rest of the plant as it was.

'Returning from a brief holiday this week I went back to the same spot and found *two* Long-eared Bats impaled on the same plant in almost the same place, about three feet above ground. The burdock stands within eighteen inches of the house wall.

'Is this a common occurrence? I had always imagined that bats were famed for their "radar" equipment, which enabled them to avoid collisions. Could they have been searching for something when they were caught?'

I have never heard of a similar instance. It is certainly not a common mishap. The bats were presumably hunting insects in the twilight when they fell foul of the burdock and perhaps in their eagerness brushed too close to the foliage, not realising that it was equipped with tiny barbed hooks. Just possibly the nearness of the wall may have confused their echo-locating equipment. But bats seldom make such mistakes.

The Spotted Horses of Somerset

I discovered the Merriott Spotted Horses by chance in 1978. I thought I was familiar with most of the breeds in the horse world, but here was one, almost on my doorstep, which I had never previously come across. It is kept alive at present by Mrs. U. R. C. R. Wallis, who then had six stallions (ten until the previous week) and about fifty mares and other horses. She is in touch with other breeders, scattered in other parts of the British Isles and a few overseas, and exports breeding animals from time to time.

The Spotted Horses are a very ancient type which seem to have slipped through the net of the breed societies. The pedigree animals are registered with the Welsh Pony and Cob Society but without reference to their spots. Some of Mrs. Wallis's horses are the size of large ponies (up to about 13 hands) but others are miniatures, and their colour is very variable. Some are white with a liberal sprinkling of black spots of varying size, Apaloosa style; others are roan or grey, with brown spots; others have only a thin peppering of spots on the flanks and none on the forequarters. A three-week-old foal which I saw showed the last-named characteristic, – a lovely little creature with grey foreparts and a dense cluster of black spots on the rear. But many of the foals are born bay-coloured, gradually changing to white with spots by the end of three years. There is a connection, some way back, with a type known as the Merriott Market Horse, which seems to have been well known in the West Country once, though so far I have very little information about it.

Mrs. Wallis is convinced that her spotted horses are descended from a prehistoric type of forest horse which once roamed wild over primeval Britain. The spotted colour pattern is typical of forest animals, such as the leopard, the dappling being useful camouflage for an animal living under a tree canopy. There is a theory that the spotted horse was at one time a totem or sacred animal for tribes who dwelt in Somerset and that associations between this type of horse and the old pagan religion lingered long in these parts, getting spotted horses a bad name with the mediaeval church. Hence spotted horses are seldom mentioned in mediaeval documents, though old pictures sometimes depict them. There is a Spotted Horse Inn at Congresbury, on the edge of the Mendips.

The Merriott horses are dainty creatures, clean-limbed and with relatively short noses. Their broad foreheads cover a braincase with a greater capacity than normal for horses of that size, and they are markedly intelligent. They are also docile, friendly and easily managed.

Further correspondence established that the Merriott Spotted Horses, once widely known as 'Merriott Markets' or 'Merriott Half-Hackneys' used to be much in demand for fast transport. From the Crewkerne and Yeovil area they used to race to Weymouth, Bridport, Lyme, Seaton or some other port with supplies of local produce and return with loads of fish. 'They went to Bristol and Salisbury markets twice a week. They also hauled heavy loads of flax to our local rope and sail mills and then transported the ropes and sails to Weymouth, to the Fleet.' One version of the origin of the name 'Halfway Hackney', by which the spotted horses were also known, is that when the horses had delivered a load to their destination they were only half-way through their journey. Turning their vehicle around with military precision, they quickly acquired another load and raced back home with it.

The men who drove the horses were sometimes known as 'Merriott tranters', presumably derived from 'transporters'. They maintained that the breed was of very ancient origin and associated it with a stock of horses maintained by the West Saxon king Ina, whose palace was situated nearby. And, although many of them were illiterate men, they used to speak of even earlier kings known otherwise only to scholars. Evidently the ancestry of both the spotted horses and their masters is lost in the mists of antiquity.

In addition to the horses of 12 or 13 hands there was also a smaller spotted animal of 11 hands or less. It had a rather long body and was known as a 'hand pony'. Its most frequent role was to carry bags of game for sportsmen.

Yet another informant told me that it was considered very unlucky to refer to a white horse or pony as anything but 'grey', and even more unlucky to mention the word 'spotted'. The spotted horses were not called 'red-spotted' or 'black-spotted' but 'roans' and 'greys'. She asked an old countryman how, then, he would describe a spotted horse to someone who had never seen one. He thought hard and eventually decided he would be happy saying, 'Marked like yours!' A neat way round the problem. But evidently the word 'spot' had come to mean something bad, and that could well have been because in the distant past the spotted animals had been sacred to a pagan religion and hence had been frowned upon by the Church.

A Seaford (Sussex) reader who saw these notes on spotted horses wrote to tell me that his brother in Australia is mad about horses and especially about spotted ones. On his occasional trips to England he spends his time looking for them and has managed to buy and export several. Some have also been brought into Australia from America, but the English horses have a reputation for being the best breeders.

One of the spotted horses that this enthusiast picked up in England on his last visit came from Sussex, and an old colleague of mine who is now living in Cumberland is breeding spotted ponies, so evidently the breed is quite well distributed.

Harvest Mice

When I was a boy I often came across the lovely little red-gold harvest mice, which were then quite common in cornfields. They were to be discovered most frequently at threshing time. My recollection is that a few were found in most wheat-ricks, when we pulled the ricks apart and threw the sheaves into the threshing drum. From the general massacre of escaping mice and rats the harvest mice were generally allowed by the men to escape, – chiefly, I think, because they were so beautiful and tiny – though, of course, the dogs were not so selective.

We also found their nests in wheat sheaves drying in the fields, though usually the mice had by then abandoned them. I have occasionally discovered nests woven around standing wheat-stalks before harvest and have marvelled at their construction, so loosely fashioned that a mouse could squeeze its way through the walls anywhere, thus dispensing with the need for an official entrance hole, and yet so strong that it could support the weight of a nestful of young ones. More often, I have found the nests in rough herbage along the edges of fields, on the fringe of hedges, and some of these I remember finding occupied.

I write in the past tense, for it is some years since I last saw a harvest mouse. From time to time I have seen their nests in the swathes of straw lying on stubbles, having passed through the threshing mechanism of a combine-harvester, though usually with very little damage. But after that traumatic experience they are, of course, empty.

The temptation is therefore to regard such an elusive and unobtrusive animal as rare, much rarer than it used to be – a conclusion which is evidently wrong. In 1973 the Mammal Society initiated a Harvest Mouse Distribution Survey, and in due course I saw the report on the survey in Wiltshire, relating chiefly to the summer of 1974.

The Survey showed that Harvest Mice are still abundant. They are nesting in the tall vegetation on the fringe of arable fields, rather than in the corn, but there are some exceptions to this rule, for in some districts 'cornfields support vast breeding colonies'. Even more congenial sites are offered by damp water-meadows and by tall roadside vegetation.

The report recorded that in November, 1974, a search was made on either side of a 200-yard stretch of road near Wilton. No fewer than 80 nests were found, of which 12 had probably been used for breeding. In the following year a search in a neighbouring field, which had been harvested, on August 10th produced 13 nests. Which indicates that the Harvest Mouse is by no means a scarce animal.

Incidentally, I was rather surprised to see under the heading of House Mouse, in this same Report, the comment:- 'Status unknown; records required.' The only record received by the compilers during the year was of six mice found in a river, having been killed in traps. Possibly everyone thinks that House Mice are so common that they are not worth recording, but apparently there is a doubt about this. Perhaps they, and not the Harvest Mice, are on the decline. They are, by the way, often confused with the Wood Mouse, or Long-tailed Field Mouse, which is larger, more brightly coloured, has a longer tail and is much commoner.

Friendly Badgers

From Hinton St. George, near Crewkerne, which is good badger country, came the following pleasant badger story:-

'On the 23rd of March we went for our usual afternoon walk, at about 3.15 p.m., across the fields. It was a sunny day with a slight south-easterly breeze. Thirty yards outside one of the woods we saw a badger feeding and scraping. We walked slowly towards it and, as we were downwind, got within ten yards. There we stood for a good twenty minutes before it noticed us. It then ambled slowly back towards the wood.

'Half an hour later we came across another one in a recently ploughed field, over a quarter of a mile from the nearest wood. Again we were downwind and were able to watch for twenty minutes or so, leaning on the park railings. As I know where many of the various setts are in the woods I wondered which one it had come from, so finally I tapped the iron railing with a stick. The badger looked up for a moment and then went on feeding. When I

tapped again it looked up again and finally squatted facing us, about fifteen yards away. We had been talking in whispers but now began to use our normal voices, but still it stayed there, until at last, finding our conversation boring, it got up and trotted slowly away.

'I have never before seen badgers out and about in mid-afternoon. By their size I would say these two were sows. Is this behaviour unusual? Perhaps they are hungry or have young to feed?'

Yes, that could be. Young badgers are generally born between late February and late April, so these two could well have had litters. The fact that the observers were downwind is important, but it would also seem certain that the local badgers are used to seeing or hearing human beings without being molested. A very satisfactory state of affairs.

Roosting Wrens

A Dorset correspondent reported, 'This evening at dusk I witnessed another species that seems to enjoy the accommodation afforded by my roof. A "cluster" of wrens entered a hole under the thatch. First, I was aware of a number of the birds flitting around the shrubs and trees near me in the garden. Some then began to gather at a spot under the eaves near a small hole between timbers. They queued up in a line along the rough stonework and on a wall nearby. There was much twittering and squabbling at the little hole, as others jumped the queue by flying down and alighting at the entrance. It took ten minutes for them all to go inside, and I had counted 32 wrens entering the hole.'

Gregarious roosting such as this by wrens has been recorded before. *The Handbook of British Birds* gives an instance of ten or more roosting together in an old coconut shell and of more than thirty in a group of old House Martins' nests. I have come across previous instances of wrens roosting in nest-boxes, and I seem to remember, though I cannot put my hands on the record at the moment, a note of a number of wrens found dead in a nest-box. The birds only behave in this way in hard weather and presumably huddle together for warmth.

The Vanished Corncrake

Watching a television programme on the Outer Hebrides I was interested to see and hear corncrakes in the hay-fields. It reminded me that not long before my time corncrakes were quite as common in the West Country as now they are in north-west Scotland, perhaps commoner. They came with the other migrating birds in spring, and in May and June the fields echoed with their gruff voices. My father said that their call was one of the most familiar sounds of the countryside, corncrakes challenging the cuckoos as they shouted across the valley.

Then they vanished. They arrived in smaller numbers with each successive spring, and finally failed to put in an appearance at all. This happened before I was old enough to take notice of such things, but not long before. I think it must have been in the first decade of the present century. My father used to speak of them as a still recent memory and was still puzzled, when I was a boy, about why they didn't come any more. In the 1930s and

1940s we saw an occasional bird or two in the cornfields at harvest-time, but these must have been birds on migration, not nesting birds. And we never heard any calling.

Several theories have been advanced to explain the disappearance of the corncrake. The one most generally favoured is that they were destroyed by modern grass-cutting machines. That seems possible, for a man riding on the seat of a horse-drawn grasscutter cannot cut around a nest in the long grass as easily as a man with a scythe. But I wonder whether the men with scythes cut around the nests? They would probably save a partridge's nest in that way if they thought they would be rewarded by the keeper, but I think they would have been more likely to take the corncrakes' eggs for supper, as happened with peewits' eggs.

Another suggestion is that with the introduction of rye-grass and red clover leys the hay-crops were ready for cutting several weeks earlier than were the old permanent pastures. Cutting the hay thus became an operation which fell in the middle of the corncrakes' nesting season. That sounds quite probable, but there were still plenty of permanent pastures being cut as hay when I was a boy, even in arable Wiltshire, and there must have been many more in the dairying districts farther west.

A third idea is that an increased use of gin-traps caught too many corncrakes in tunnels, constructed for vermin in gaps in hedgerows. The secretive corncrakes naturally used those tunnels. But I believe that gin-traps were in pretty common use throughout most of the nineteenth century.

Perhaps all three factors played a part. And the fortunes of species of wild creatures do fluctuate regardless of the action of human beings. The recent expansion of collared doves right across Europe, to become common in every corner of Britain, has had little if anything to do with any human activity.

The disappearance of another bird shown in the same television programme is more easily explained. That was the Wheatear, which when I was a boy was one of the common summer visitors to the Wiltshire downs. Almost any year in the late 1920s and early 1930s I could have taken a visitor to a dozen nests within two or three miles of my home. Now I doubt if there is even one, though occasional wheatears still turn up on migration.

The explanation here is the ploughing-up of the downland. Wheatears used to nest in old rabbit-holes, and there is now nowhere for them to make their nests.

By way of contrast, the peewit or lapwing has recorded a success story. Here is a bird which should have been particularly vulnerable to the disturbance caused by modern methods of agriculture. In the days of horse-propelled cultivations horsemen would keep an eye open for peewits' nests in late March and April. From the early nests they would take eggs and either fry them for breakfast or sell them. There was a ready market. The later nests they would move over to the strip of field they had just cultivated, and the watchful mother bird would take note and resume incubation. I doubt whether many tractor-drivers practise the same consideration. Logically, the peewit ought to have become as rare as that other ground-nesting bird with which it was frequently associated, the stone-curlew. Yet it flourishes. There are as many peewits about in winter as ever. It is strange.

Familiarity Breeds Contempt

Watching the flying display from a vantage-point on the perimeter of Yeovilton airfield on the Fleet Air Arm's Air Day I was intrigued to see a kestrel hovering over the smooth grass while the jets thundered deafeningly overhead. The bird, intent on detecting the slightest movement in the grass below, took not the slightest notice, even when one plane hurtled past apparently only a few yards above it.

Nearby was a party of wagtails, evidently on migration, and they too were apparently oblivious to all the commotion. But they took fright when parachutists came floating down towards them. Presumably they suspected these must be some new species of giant hawk.

When, in accordance with the mixed farming economy of the past, we kept poultry of virtually every kind on our farm, an uproar among the chicken, ducks, geese and turkeys in the farmyard usually implied that a hawk had passed overhead. And I vividly recall the commotion among the turkeys when the sweep pushed his brush out of the top of the farmhouse chimney.

Vulnerable Young Birds

My garden in mid-June seems full of young birds. It was just 38 days from the time when a pair of mistle-thrushes started building their nest in the honeysuckle over our lounge window to the date (June 5th) when the young ones flew. There is a wren's nest, with young about ready to fly, in the dense tangle of stalks of another honeysuckle on the back wall; and in a cavity in the stone wall of the woodshed a pair of great tits is rearing a very large family. Starlings occupy an old woodpeckers' hole in a tree in the orchard, and two pairs of sparrows, a pair of blue tits, several chaffinches and blackbirds and a pair of great spotted woodpeckers come foraging on our lawn all day and every day. The rooks, jackdaws and magpies which nest in the tall trees just over the garden wall are ever with us.

The rate at which these nestlings grow is prodigious. From hatching to flight from the nest is only about a fortnight, and the parent birds stuff food into the babies so assiduously that the difference in size is visible daily. One cannot help but feel compassion for the virtually helpless youngsters on their first days out of the nest. They know nothing of the dangers that await them, from cats to cars, and untold numbers of them fail to last beyond the first week.

The other day a sparrow-hawk actually came into our garden and took a young blackbird from the lawn. I happened to go outdoors just at that moment, a coincidence which sent the hawk scurrying into the shrubbery, where it was followed by the protesting parents, but it did not release its victim, and I did not attempt to interfere. This was one occasion when I did not allow my heart to rule my head. The hawk needed to eat, too, and small birds were its natural food, just as lambs are ours.

I remember how one of my daughters, when she was perhaps six or seven years old, came crying to me that the cat had a mouse and 'the big boys were teasing her with it.' When I went out to see them, the boys gave me the mouse, which was still alive, so I let it escape. My daughter's tears were unabated. 'You stupid thing,' she sobbed. 'Now the poor pussy hasn't got any dinner!'

It depends on the point of view. From the viewpoint of a hawk, a young mistle-thrust is a scrumptious dish of protein. But I am glad my house birds escaped. I have seen them since, flying around the trees.

The time at which the young birds leave the nest is apparently determined by a precise inner mechanism. When the moment comes they are impelled to go. I remember an incident which occurred some years ago, when a pair of blue tits nested in a nesting-box in our garden. Having watched their progress through the whole process of incubation and fledging we were upset when they started to leave the nest in the middle of a heavy thunderstorm. If they had waited for only a couple of hours all would have been well. As it was the heavy rain battered and chilled them, as well as confusing their anxious parents, and most of them succumbed. Obviously they were not choosing the moment of departure but were obeying an impulse not understood by us.

Quail

In August, 1976 a naturalist friend who lives near Ilminster wrote to tell me of a Quail nesting in a field just outside Hemyock. A farmer found it while combining a field of barley. He spotted the bird in the stubble and thought at first it was a young pheasant. Then, as the bird did not move far, he went nest-hunting and found what he was looking for 'deep in a tangle of rough grass which was growing on the site of a hedge he had grubbed out last winter, before drilling the barley. The seed hadn't taken well just there, and so both combine-harvester and baler had missed the nest. The farmer then remembered that he had heard a strange bird calling on several occasions recently.'

My friend managed to get some photos and heard the cock call several times to the sitting female. 'She is so tiny,' he commented. 'When settled on the cup-shaped nest she crouches down almost level with the soil surface and then rapidly draws the surrounding grasses above her to form an effective canopy.' The eggs were very small and coloured much like those of a moorhen. They hatched on July 24th; and by the next day the chicks had wandered off over the stubbles and could not be found.

Quail were also heard in several other places in Somerset that summer. In June birds were heard calling at Bagborough, on the edge of the Quantocks, and at Beer Crocombe.

In the 1930s I came to know this bird quite well, for a pair nested for several consecutive years in a derelict field adjoining our farm in south Wilts. As with the Hemyock pair, they chose a site in coarse, grassy vegetation. I remember that one year the nest had thirteen eggs. After the young had hatched, the female packed the egg-shells neatly inside each other before leaving the nest. I understand this is a Quail custom.

Later, for several years after the war, I used to hear Quail calling in our valley, along harvest-time. Their piping call is sometimes written, 'Wet-my-lips, wet-my-lips', which reproduces it fairly accurately. But I haven't heard it now for perhaps fifteen or twenty years, and the field where the birds nested pre-war is now submerged by bungalows and suburban gardens.

The last Quail's nest I found was in India, five or six years ago. A different species of Quail from ours, I think, but not so very different. I saw the bird suddenly take wing and, walking across, had no difficulty in finding the nest. Then I wished I hadn't, for an Indian with me marked it for future use. I think he wanted to try to trap the male bird, for Quail-fighting.

Octo, the Molluscicide

When staying overnight with a Wiltshire friend in September, 1978, he mentioned the snails which infested his garden and which, he said, were so numerous that at nights they were 'like a layer of pebbles on the lawn'. So after dark we went out with a torch and there, sure enough, were the snails, just like a bed of cobblestones. It would have been impossible to walk without stepping on dozens of them.

Only once before have I ever seen snails in such numbers and that was years ago, when I was a boy and we had a plague of snails in the garden. We also had a pet Aylesbury duck named Octo, so-called because she was the only survivor from a brood of eight ducklings. We rightly surmised that the snails were hiding by day in the rockery, so, over a period of several weeks, we dismantled that rockery stone by stone, shifting some of them at a set hour each evening. Octo happened to be there on the first night and took immediate advantage of what was going on. Thereafter she was ready well before the appointed time, all eager to start. One of us had to hold her back while we moved the larger stones, in case one fell on her; then, the moment we let her go, she was in among those snails, gobbling them up as fast as she could swallow. Modern gardeners are familiar with insecticides, fungicides, molluscicides and the rest. Although we did not know the term then, Octo was the most effective molluscicide I have ever come across. I could do with her now.

Badgers Eating Corn-cobs

During one seed-time a Stalbridge reader was discussing with me the trouble he had had in the previous year with the sweetcorn in his garden. In mid-September. when the stalks were five feet high and when he had just harvested four delicious cobs, the plot was completely ravaged overnight by something which broke down the stalks, stripped the covering off the cobs and gnawed them. As the ground was hard and dry there were no footprints. Now he wanted to take precautions against a repetition of the disaster, but what were the culprits?

As the cobs were gnawed it cannot have been a bird; birds cannot gnaw. A rat, rabbit or hare would have gnawed half through the base, allowed the stalk to topple over and then helped itself to the cobs, but there was no sign of gnawing at the base. So that brings us to some large animal. Roe deer? Sheep?

Sheep are probably out, for they would have left traces of wool. Roe deer are a distinct possibility, but now badgers have been suggested. Would a badger eat corn cobs? Yes, I said, I imagined it would, knowing from experience how omnivorous badgers are.

The mystery naturally prompted a number of readers to write or telephone to enlighten me on the identity of the culprits. All agreed that they were badgers. A Yeovil reader said he had actually caught them at work in his garden, so there could be no doubt about it.

A Bourton gardener assured me he had been troubled in this way for the past two seasons and quoted a paragraph he wrote for the Plessey house magazine, *Throop News*. After a lot of trouble he managed to grow four reasonably successful rows of sweet corn and was just anticipating a feast, the cobs being at the ideal stage, when he found the entire plot flattened and only the bare husks left. A large hole in the hedge, leading to a sett on adjoining property, provided good circumstantial evidence. A Dorchester reader told me that a farmer in the district lost a quarter of an acre of maize to badgers last year. Everyone was impressed at the badger's ability to judge when the corn is just right.

My Bourton correspondent wondered whether there is any rustic lore about it and suggested something on the following lines:-

'When Brock tayke corne in September they dew saye,
    It'll mean bags of bewze on Christmas Day!'

It's a happy thought, but sweetcorn and maize cobs haven't been known in England long enough to produce any folk lore. That implies, too, of course, that they haven't been here long enough for badgers to have acquired any inherited knowledge about the crop. Which makes the fact that these instances have been happening simultaneously in a number of places even more extraordinary.

By some means, and it is almost certainly by scent, the badgers are able to deduce that something attractively edible is available at the top of those brittle stems. The experience of a Bridport reader may therefore be significant. After suffering not one but two visitations, with an interval of two nights between, which stripped not only the ripe but, on the second occasion, the unripe cobs as well, he splashed creosote all around his garden to prevent damage to other crops. No further damage occurred. It may be that the badgers were interested only in the corn, but, alternatively, and this could be important, it may be that the strong smell of the creosote smothered that of the other vegetables. I would think that creosote is well worth trying. And if the badgers' behaviour of recent summers is anything to go by, we shall have ample opportunity for testing any remedies we can think of.

I am not, by the way, surprised at the badgers' newfound liking for corn cobs. There are three notable omnivorous animals – pigs, badgers and Man. When, years ago, I had a pet badger, Barney, we used to scrape the dinner plates into his dish – potatoes, meat scraps, vegetables, gravy, custard, blackberry tart, cheese rind, biscuit crumbs – all mixed together, and he scoffed the lot. No finicky feeder, that badger!

A Deer Shamming Death

Early in 1979 a Sturminster Newton reader commented on the large numbers of roe deer roaming the countryside nowadays.

'The largest number I have seen up to now,' he wrote, 'was in February, when walking on Bulbarrow (the highest point of the Dorset Heights). In the course of about two hours we saw a total of forty roe deer. Twenty-five of them were in the same small field, some lying down but most grazing like a herd of cattle.'

Another reader, from Shaftesbury, enquired whether it is unusual to see a deer shamming death. 'About a month ago, when I was walking in fields below Shaftesbury, my dog put up a young deer, which bounded off to the left. It moved unusually slowly and scraped under a barbed-wire fence instead of jumping it. A few moments later another deer came out, moving to the right and followed by the dog (a six-year-old Labrador). Despite being chased, it too was moving very slowly and, what has never happened before, the dog was catching up on it. I ran after them to the edge of a copse, and when I got there the dog was coming out, pretending to be interested in something else. Looking into the wood, I saw the deer sprawling motionless on the ground between a couple of trees.

Like the dog, I didn't quite know what to do. From where I was standing, about ten yards away, the deer appeared to be breathing gently. I wondered whether it was shamming dead or whether it had stunned itself by bumping against one of the trees. I decided to inform the owner of the wood, but when I returned about an hour later the deer had gone.'

This is certainly puzzling behaviour. I have turned over in my mind the various possibilities and have rejected the idea that the second deer was shamming. I think the likeliest explanation is that these were bucks who had just shed their horns, which they do at that time of the year. It is apparently a traumatic experience, and these animals were feeling the stress. What they wanted to do was to lie down for half-an-hour, undisturbed by humans or dogs, and they were all right again.

Birds Like Red Flowers

I received the following query:- 'Of a row of runner beans I planted this year, one half was red-flowered, the other half white-flowered. Most of the early flowers on both lots dropped off, because of the drought, and birds picked off most of the later red flowers, even those at the tops of the poles. But the white flowers they left alone, with the result that these plants produced a cascade of flowers, which set a good crop. If birds do prefer red to white, I shall plant white in future.'

It is a fact that birds are attracted by bright colours. I would say this observation and the inference are correct. But there is just a slight doubt. Why is it that bottles, set up on sticks to keep pigeons off cabbage plants, have to be red? Or is this an old wives' tale?

So What were these Mice up to?

A Gillingham (Dorset) reader, asked whether I could suggest any explanation for the following episode.

'Last year, having been pestered by mice eating newly-planted peas and beans, I deposited several large jam jars containing small quantities of *Warfarin* along the rows. I chose narrow-necked jars and shook the poison to the lower end so that the birds, dogs and cats could not get at the stuff. It did the trick. I had excellent germination and subsequent crops. I picked up the jars, some of them still containing *Warfarin*, and put them under the staging of my greenhouse.

'When in November I dug up my dahlia tubers and prepared to stack them under the staging I was astonished to find that each jar neck was filled completely with small stones, straw and paper, so that it was impossible for anything to get in. It seemed that something had gone to considerable lengths to prevent any creature from getting at the contents. I replaced two of the jars behind the dahlia tubers, after cleaning them out, and several days later found that the blocking had been repeated.

'After Christmas I discovered mice had been nibbling apples in a tray in a shed. I set a couple of traps and also placed a small saucer of *Warfarin* alongside. Two days later I caught a mouse in a trap but was surprised to find that the saucer had been covered with fluff and rubbish, thus concealing the poison.'

I can hardly believe that they would be altruistic enough or farseeing enough to try to protect each other in this way. But it does seem that they acted deliberately. I can only suggest that the smell of the poison was in some way offensive to them and that they covered it instinctively.

Several readers wrote to report similar instances. The following letter came from Somerset:-

'A large store of apples in my garage last November was attracting huge numbers of mice so I decided to use *Warfarin* on them. Having dealt with them I used a surplus in the greenhouse. I placed one container of poison on a shelf and one on the central floor space, which was covered with loose gravel. Next morning I was amazed to find the container on the floor filled to overflowing with gravel, and there was also some gravel in the pot on the shelving. I was so interested that I repeated the process five times, and on each occasion the containers were filled with gravel. At this stage the poison supply was exhausted, so I decided to leave the mice alone. I am still wondering whether the mice were acting in a spirit of self-preservation or enjoying a little entertainment – to see which could put most stones in the pot!

A Tollard Royal (Wiltshire) reader said that he too had known a mouse cover poison with thick sticks and rubbish. Indeed, the stuff it used was so large that he suspected a rat, until the mouse was caught. He has also known rats to drop pebbles and small potatoes on the plate of a rat gin, carrying them some distance to do so. On the other hand, they have carried off small plastic trays of poison, presumably to eat at leisure.

Flycatchers in a Hurry

In 1976 I was intrigued, once again, by the activities of a pair of Spotted Flycatchers in our garden. Apart from an odd bird on passage, we had seen none here until July 8th, when several arrived. A few days later I found, to my surprise, that a pair of them were making a nest in a forsythia bush against the house wall. Nest-building occupied only a day or two, and soon the bird was incubating. I kept clear, so as not to give the site away to marauding squirrels and magpies, but eventually four young birds were visible, peering over the top of the nest. They flew on the morning of August 3rd. So, from the time we first saw this pair to the time the young birds left the nest was not quite four weeks. The parents may have been around for a day or two before we spotted them, but they certainly didn't start building the nest until July 10th. Quick work.

This must have been a second brood, I feel sure, for the parents would hardly have been in the country until the first week of July without nesting. And it is rather surprising that they chose a completely new site for this second venture.

In Praise of Bulls

Several readers asked me why I chose the subject of bulls for my 1977 Christmas book, *Bulls Through the Ages*. Maybe it was sympathy for a much maligned and maltreated animal. Shire horses are popular because they combine enormous strength with immense docility. They are indeed 'gentle giants'. Lions are likewise attractive because, in addition to being virile and allegedly fierce, they look like oversized pussycats. Bulls are massive and masculine but suffer from a reputation for savagery without the redeeming features of either the heavy horse or the lion.

The trouble is that people in general are afraid of bulls. So they believe the worst about them and shut them in small concrete pens, or put rings through their noses and tether them to posts which allow them to move only in circles, and then look at them from the other side of the fence and say, 'My! don't they look fierce!' But, in fact, a bull under natural circumstances is an attractive and efficient patriarch of a herd. When running free with his harem he is as gentle with the calves as any human father is with his offspring, though always ready to do battle if danger threatens. That is the essence of his tragedy. He is too well able to look after them and himself, so he has to be confined and restricted.

I had charge of the village bull for, I suppose, about ten or fifteen years, during which four or five bulls passed through my hands. Because of the lay-out of our farm they had to be kept in a pen, though I would have much preferred to give them free range. I never had one I was afraid of, and there was one who would allow a child to sit on his back. Other farmers have demonstrated that there is no difficulty in training a bull to carry a rider on his back.

Some breeds, of course, are more amenable than others, the dairy breeds being less reliable than the beef ones. I would consider it foolish to enter a field containing a strange bull without carrying a stick. But those who have had the care of considerable numbers of bulls put the incidence of 'rogue' individuals at between one in forty and one in eighty. The human race probably produces a higher proportion of rogues than that.

COUNTRY FOLK

Hunting the Deer

Edward Step, writing in 1921, said that in southern England roe deer were to be found only in parts of Dorset and in the New Forest. 'Even so,' he commented, 'quiet ramblers in the thicker woods and plantations of the New Forest have a slender prospect of seeing it.' Now a quiet rambler through almost any wood in the West Country would be unlucky not to see one. And motorists along our country lanes at night (for this deer is nocturnal) often catch sight of one in their headlights. I must have seen dozens over the past year.

At one time the roe deer was extinct throughout most of England, surviving only in the northernmost counties. Then

certain landowners in the south, starting with Lord Portar-
lington at Milton Abbas (Dorset) introduced some from Europe
into their woods, and from there the deer spread till now they are
widespread and plentiful. Towards the end of the year roe deer are
shedding their antlers. The bucks tend to go off on their own,
seeking the highest ground in their territory, and until they start
to grow new antlers they keep out of sight and look miserable.

Fallow deer are not as common as they used to be. Back in the
1920s and 1930s our farm in south Wiltshire was over-run by
them. Herds of thirty or forty often used to come by night to raid
our mangold-heaps, scraping aside the thatch with their hooves.
By day they would retire to inaccessible forests, and fences would
not keep them away, so virtually the only means of protection
that farmers knew was to set wire snares (nooses of wire clothes'-
lines!) in hedgerow gaps through which they obviously passed.
Very few were ever caught, though.

I have been turning over some of the records of Cranborne
Chase, a region in which throughout most of history deer (mostly
fallow in the past, though now roe as well) have been abundant
and where deer-hunting and deer-poaching have been notorious. In Ashmore parish all the cultivated land had to be
enclosed by a deer fence five feet high, as had also copses of wood
less than three years old. Evidently the deer were always trying to
creep through the fences to get at the growing crops, and the
parishioners used to set nooses in the gaps they made. The keepers
who were supposed to protect the deer used to be induced indoors
to enjoy a glass of ale with some householder while the neighbours
were examining their snares. By day the deer would feed with the
sheep on the open downs and were often almost as numerous as
the sheep. It was in the evening that they attempted to break into
the corn-land.

Until about 1800 the Ashmore people enjoyed an organised
deer hunt on Easter Monday. At other seasons they just helped
themselves. Nor was deer-poaching, or deer-hunting, confined to
farm labourers. Farmers and even gentry indulged in it. William
Chafin, writing in 1818, tells a story of a pillar of local society who
was also leader of the band. He used to go to church with his music
books under his arm and with nooses for deer-snaring hidden
between the sheets of music.

One Sunday in August, when talking to the lord of the manor
on the way home from church he happened to see a herd of deer

which, annoyed by flies, were taking cover in a detached coppice. When the conversation was ended and his companion was out of sight he made his way to the far side of the copse and set snares in every pathway leading from it. Then he returned to the opposite side and threw pebbles into the wood. The deer, of course, retreated to the far side and attempted to return to the main forest. Strolling back to examine his nooses he found he had caught three fine bucks.

He cut their throats, dragged the carcases to an old sawpit in the woods, paunched them and threw them in, covering them with leaves. Then he climbed a leafy oak and there settled down to read a book of classics until it was time for the evening band practice. He and his musical team collected the carcases in a cart after dark.

The very abundance of deer in the Chase at that time encouraged poaching. In a hard winter, says an Ashmore historian, they perished by thousands. In one forest walk alone 500 young deer died in the winter of 1825, and the smell of the rotting bodies kept woodmen away from their work. The deer stock was farmed though evidently not culled. Although fences kept them out of woods less than three years old (meaning woods that were cut at regular intervals for hurdle-making and other underwood crafts), in the third year creeps were made to allow the fawns to go in.

Although, as is quite well known, frequent battles between keepers and poachers in time developed into virtually open war, the keepers themselves were not averse to taking a deer from time to time. Chafin tells of a venerable keeper who, having sworn, as he was required to annually, to the truth of his tally of deer killed and disposed of during the year, confessed privately that he had to perjure himself '... for he could have no peace nor content at home unless he made his old Jane's frying-pan hiss now and then; for she could not live without venison, having been so long used to it.'

I was prompted to turn to these old books again through reading of the activities of poachers and cattle-rustlers recently in the West Country. The technique nowadays apparently is to drive a car into a previously selected field on the edge of a wood on a dark night and plug any deer that appear in the car headlights. The carcases are taken to a waiting van, which is miles away within a few minutes. If deer fail to appear and sheep are present, that is just too bad. Sheep carcases are just as saleable.

Local poachers are generally known or suspected, and a kind of guerrilla war is waged between them and authority. Blood-chilling tales go the rounds about encounters that are alleged to have taken place, but I am never sure whether they are to be believed. Even more sinister and difficult to counter, however, are the activities of urban poachers from the big cities. Modern motorways have made much of the West Country easily accessible to them. They are completely ruthless and motivated only by the desire for a quick profit.

A Rolling Hedge

In the New Forest the other day I was asked whether I knew what a 'rolling hedge' was. No, I did not. It was a device used by commoners in the old days to encroach on the open common land. Having observed that he was likely to get away with filching another plot adjoining his holding, the commoner would plant a hedge around it, with a ditch on the far side to protect the hedge from grazing stock in the conventional manner. After the hedge had stood with no objections from anyone for a year or two the man would plant another on the far side of the ditch. Again if there were no objections he would dig a ditch on the far side of this new hedge. He would then fill in the first ditch and uproot the first hedge. By this process, continued for several decades, he would eventually enclose quite a substantial paddock – an acre or two for nothing!

Another feature of some of the older New Forest cottages and even of larger houses is a kind of leanto annexe to the kitchen, often rounded. Today it can serve any one of a number of purposes, from a larder to a kind of observation nook, but it began life as a pigsty. Forest law prohibited the erection of a separate building, but many a commoner rightly argued that no-one would notice or object to a pigsty tacked on to the cottage.

Lost Villages

In a Canadian magazine I read the lament of a writer who was deploring the disappearance of the rural way of life in Canada. A hundred years ago, he says, the population of Canada was 75% rural; now it is getting on for 75% urban. The farms went broke and were abandoned between the wars; community halls were vandalised and demolished; the railway stations were closed down, as were the general stores, the local garage and the country school. 4,000 village schools have closed in the province of Saskatchewan alone since the end of the second world war.

He went out one day, about twenty years ago, to interview the inhabitants of a village which was about to be obliterated to make room for a big international airport. They found an old woman. 'In answer to my first and only query she damned us all to hell – me, the photographer and all the forces of the modern world that could be so brutal as to pull off such a stunt and destroy her ancestral home. ... I know how she felt.'

So do I. By coincidence a great-uncle of mine, who, as I have mentioned in one of my books, emigrated to Canada in the 1800s and persuaded many young men from his corner of the West Country to follow him, eventually lost his farm to Calgary airport. But the alternative might have been slow death.

When my son was married, to a girl in a rural community in Manitoba, he and his wife went to live first in what was called a 'township' near where he was working. Perhaps seventy or eighty years earlier the place had been founded with, no doubt, high hopes for the future. It was a station on the prairie railway, alongside which stood a towering grain elevator. It was given an impressive name and accorded a place on the map. But when he went to live there in 1971 it was a bleak, lonely outpost of some half-a-dozen timber houses on the treeless prairie. A small general store was on its last legs; trains seldom if ever stopped; no church, community hall or school survived. Obtaining the tenancy of a house at a reasonable rent was easy, for no-one wanted to live there. The few remaining residents were glad to get a new neighbour, but, understandably, he did not stay there long.

In England we are so used to seeing communities grow that to observe the reverse phenomenon is a strange experience. Yet if, like the Canadian countryside, our villages depended only on the agricultural population a parallel decline would be commonplace. It is only because most of our villages are near enough to towns to be used by commuters with cars that they continue to maintain or increase their population. Set them in a wild countryside 200 miles from the nearest big town, and, like the Canadian 'township' similarly situated, they would soon wilt and die.

Come to think of it, there *have* been instances of West Country villages dying even within my lifetime. Imber, on Salisbury Plain, is an obvious example, but that was subject to special circumstances, having been forcibly evacuated to make room for the Army. But between the wars I remember visiting the lost village of Snap, on the downs near Marlborough. People then alive could recall when Snap had a dozen or two houses, a post box and a Baptist chapel. Then, in the agricultural depression, the land around it was taken over and run on a ranching basis; there was no work for the men to do; and gradually they drifted away.

In one of my earliest books I wrote:- 'Walking down the flint-cobbled lane to Snap in July, 1948, I found it difficult to know when I had reached the village. Only here and there were traces of the old walls visible. A stranger would pass it by without suspecting its story, if it were not for the apple trees and the big walnut tree that still shade the long grass. I saw a thrush beating a snail against the foundation of a cottage wall, a thrush that no doubt was a lineal descendant of birds which sang to children playing there fifty years ago. ... If a village is as easy to kill as this, how many villages must have lived and died on our downs in the days before written history?'

Well, I know sufficiently more about the matter now to appreciate that there must have been hundreds. Up to the end of 1968 2,263 sites of deserted and 'lost' villages had been located in Britain, of which well over 300 were in our western shires. No doubt many others have been located since then. Most of them were mediaeval, it is true, but there were others which lingered down almost into the realm of living memory. I remember that, when living in the Salisbury district, I became involved in trying to locate a village named Warminster Green, which had existed up to at least the middle of the nineteenth century. We combed the countryside around Warminster in vain but eventually found someone who remembered that there had been a village of that name on the edge of the New Forest, just west of Downton. It had evidently been quite a flourishing little place, with a non-conformist chapel, but within a hundred years it had been so completely forgotten that even its site was unknown.

And that, I fear, would be the fate of great numbers of our West Country villages were it not for the much-maligned motor-car and for the 'suburban' residents who, because of the motor-car, are enabled to live in them. Even now the closure of village schools, the curtailment of rural bus services and the decay of community life are making some of them perilously vulnerable.

Another approach is ventilated by a reader whose memory takes him back to the 1920s, when cottage rents in villages were 2/6 to 4/6 a week.

The entire parish belonged to one big estate-owner, who at that time came under pressure from the tenants to sell them the houses they were occupying. The householders said that most of them had already paid the initial cost of the houses in rent – which may well have been true, for the cottages had been erected in the nineteenth century or earlier. In the end the estate gave way and allowed the tenants to purchase their houses at the bargain prices of about £100 apiece.

Not long afterwards the influx of holiday-makers began, and the village, being not too far from the sea, became popular. The visitors liked the place and began to enquire about buying property, for week-end use or retirement, and were willing to pay fantastic prices, say, £400 or £500 per house. Those villagers who fancied themselves as businessmen snapped up the offers quickly and crowed about making 400% or 500% profit.

Later they were not quite as cock-a-hoop when they saw their more cautious neighbours, who had kept their houses, selling them at £2,000 or even £4,000 each. But at that rate few could resist the blandishments of the newcomers, and some years before the property price explosion occurred in 1972 and 1973 almost every dwelling-place in the parish had passed into the hands of "outlanders".

But now those same cottages, modernised and smartened up, it is true, change hands at £20,000 or £25,000, and the present members of the old village families are aghast. The children and grandchildren of those villagers who agitated so effectively to be allowed to buy their property are now agitating with equal vigour to persuade the estate to put up cottages for them to rent! 'Or else,' they say, 'these newcomers, who pay more than we can afford, will drive us all out. There's nowhere for our children to live when they get married.'

The estate-owner, who remembers how the present situation arose, smiles wryly.

Homespun Philosophy

Sorting through some old note-books at the end of the year, I came across one in which, many years ago, I jotted down old proverbs, saws and bits of homespun philosophy as they came my way. Some of them hit the mark so neatly that they are worth passing on.

'There's one thing that most people are loaded with and are delighted to give away to anyone who will take it, and that is – advice.'

'If you tell a man two stories, one showing a neighbour in a good light and the other showing the neighbour in a bad light, it's the bad one which will come back to you before the end of the week.'

The following from a good breeder of pedigree cattle:-

'I was a very good trader, for when I had a beast I liked well I could never find anyone who liked him better than I did.'

From a rascally old poacher I used to know:-

'I owe a lot to my mother. I had to learn to be sharp to keep her from finding out I wasn't so wonderful as she thought I was.'

A comment from an old preacher:-

'The Lord loves bald-headed men. It says in the Good Book that even the hairs on our head are numbered, and see what a lot of book-keeping I'm saving him!'

'It's better to get home safe with a light load than to get stuck on the road with a heavy one.'

'People who try hard to be important, always succeed in the end. They're always the most important person present at their own funeral.'

'For a long time I couldn't understand how it was I had so much better an opinion of myself than other people did. Then I saw that

I was judging myself by my best efforts, whereas they were judging me by my worst. And I saw, too, that I was doing the same to them.'

'If you manage to reach the age of eighty, stop worrying. Statistics show that comparatively few people die after the age of eighty.'

'The older I get, the better I used to be.' (That sounds something like Mark Twain, who said that when he was fourteen he couldn't bear to have his father around, the old man was so ignorant: but by the time he was eighteen it was surprising how much the old man had learned.)

'Learn to be self-sufficient. Then when you're alone, you'll be in good company.'

'Good luck wears many disguises. One of its favourites is hard work.'

'The easiest way to make mistakes is to mess about with something you don't understand.'

'There are two sorts of ignorance. Once is not knowing things; the other is knowing things that just aren't so. The second is the more dangerous by a long way.'

'Birch trees sometimes survive by bending before a gale which uproots the oaks.'

The following West Country proverb used to be widely known:-

'The best recommendation for a good thatcher is that he can sleep well on a stormy night.'

But one cynical person to whom I quoted it commented:

'Perhaps that was because the rascal had done his job so badly that he knew he would have a couple of months' work ahead, replacing the thatch which the wind had blown off!'

When someone remarked about a certain person that he hadn't done any harm in his life, a shrewd old boy remarked,

'What use is that? If he hasn't done any good, all he's been doing is filling up space.'

'A wise man knows when to stop. A wiser man knows when not to start.'

'Talk is cheap; ideas dear. It isn't often you find the two together.'

'The early bird catches the worm. Moral – don't be an early worm.'

'A wealthy man is, at the end, remembered not by what he had but by how he got it and how he used it.'

'If a tolerant understanding is what you need, go to a man of many faults.'

'Looking back, it isn't things that you've done that you oughtn't to have done that you regret most; it's the things that you could have done but didn't do.'

From a plumber:

'Most of the customers who phone me want the job done the day before yesterday.'

'Grass grows by inches. It is destroyed by feet.'

An old widow lady in very poor circumstances who, as so often happens with the very poor, kept remarkably cheerful, said,

'I thanks the Lord every day that I wasn't born before tea.'

She loved her cup of tea, and she had read somewhere that there was a time before tea was known in England.

'When the river overflows and deposits four inches of slimy mud on your carpets and on the carpets of all your neighbours' houses as well, it never seems as bad as when your house is the only one that's flooded and all the neighbours escape.'

'A person who really understands tribulation is the housewife who sees the clothes'-prop break, her clean washing dumped on the garden, and the cat walking over it with muddy paws.'

And do you remember that other astute comment made by Mark Twain:

'A cat who has once sat on a hot stove, never makes the same mistake again. But she will never sit on a cold stove, either.'

That doesn't exhaust the list by any means, but to finish with I must include the story of the man, notorious for his tall yarns, who described how he was chased by a bull across Salisbury Plain. The bull was gaining on him; he could feel its hot breath on his neck, but in the nick of time he managed to reach a tree and shin up it.

One of his listeners objected, 'But there aren't any trees on Salisbury Plain.'

The story-teller fixed him with a steady eye.

'By God! there *had* to be. Or else I wouldn't be here, would I?' he said.

Later someone treated me to a good up-to-date one.

'The way this country is being run is like a farmer neglecting the ploughing and sowing and putting all his men on hedge-trimming.'

I like that one.

The Travelling Dentist

Some notes of West Country fairs prompted a letter from a reader at Kilmington who wrote:-

'I remember till just before the First World War seeing in Devon a travelling dentist, operating on a horse-drawn waggon. Besides the dentist's usual apparatus there was a man with a big drum, which was beaten furiously while the patient had a tooth (or teeth) extracted. The horse was not left in the shafts during the operation, and the banging of the drum was to drown the screams of the patient. Invariably a hearty farm-labourer, he told his pals "It didn't 'urt a bit" and joined the crowd to watch the next victim. The price was threepence a tooth.'

Becoming Accepted

A Yetminster reader wondered how long it takes for a family to be accepted in West Country villages and how long they remain 'outsiders'. He quoted an instance from Kent where, many years ago, someone asked an old resident of Lydd whether his neighbour was also a Lydd man.

'No, he's not. He's a furriner.'

'But he's lived here all his life, hasn't he?'

'Aye, and his father too. But his grandfather came from Ashford.'

Which reminds me that when I was a boy there was a subtle difference between the three local families who had lived in our village for many generations and the others whose roots were shallower. One of the latter category had been there so long that it had split into several households only very distantly related, but it was still remembered that once they had 'come from up Andover way'. In later years I discovered that they had moved into the village in the year 1801!!

No sugar for Wesleyans

An old couple with whom I had tea remarked when I refused sugar, 'Be you a Wesleyan, then?'

Apparently about two hundred years ago the Wesleyans of Cornwall barred sugar on the grounds that it was grown by slave labour in the West Indies and carried in ships which also engaged in the slave trade. So anybody who says No to sugar is still automatically classed as a Wesleyan! Still, it's not an uncomplimentary distinction!

The Patriarch

I feel I would rather have liked to meet the old farmer of Tavistock of whom Mrs. Bray, the rector's wife there, wrote in 1833. She gives him a glowing build-up to begin with, saying that he was 'strictly honest in his dealings relative to business, and would pay even a farthing in settling an account, rightly saying that a farthing debt was as much due as a pound. He was also an excellent master to his labourers; and such a lover was he of all the country customs that, while he lived, he might be considered as the representative of old manners and past times. Every festival throughout the year was duly observed by him and his household; and his men working on the farm had their full share of all the sports. No house displayed such an abundance of shrove cakes; May-day had its honours; and as Christmas was crowned with evergreens, the yule-logs were noble, and roast-beef and plum-puddings feasted the poor; whilst all the games and frolics of that season were celebrated with the honours their antiquity required ...'

So far, so good, but she continues,

'There was nothing to be said against this liberal old farmer, excepting that he considered himself a profound theologian; controverted the doctrines of the Established Church, and in his advanced years chose to give a practical example of patriarchal living that scandalized all the neighbourhood.'

Apparently he came to consider that his life-style was so like that of the Biblical patriarchs that he was entitled to behave in every respect as they did. Modelling himself on Abraham, he announced he was going to take his wife's maid as a hand-maid and raise a family by her.

His friends tried to dissuade him.

'I'm not doing anything wrong,' he told them. 'I'm only doing that Abraham did.'

'What about your wife, whom you've lived with for more than forty years?'

'Well, she still has first place of honour in the house, as Sarah did. I'm not turning her out.'

His wife, however, had other ideas, as most wives would. She went off to live with a married daughter, who evidently resided in the same parish. The old man accepted this but made a point of sending her, almost daily, some of the best of the produce of the farm. Apparently the hand-maid, whose name was Mary, had the job of taking it round.

The farmer then announced that his hand-maid was going to bear him five children, just as Sarah's hand-maid bore for Abraham. And he was right. She produced three boys and two girls. The children, he declared, were to be brought up 'on his wife's knees', as happened with Abraham's children by his hand-maid, but whether his wife was willing to co-operate to that extent is not recorded. The children were named Abraham, Isaac, Jacob, Sarah and, when the last one arrived, it should have been Rebecca. However, the hand-maid wanted it named after herself, Mary, and the old man relented to that extent. It was a good name, he said, and he trusted that the little girl would grow up worthy of it.

Unfortunately, that is where the story ends. We feel we would like to know more. What happened when the old father died, his family still young? Did the old wife take them under her wing, or were they thrown out, like Hagar and Ishmael? And what did the complaisant hand-maid feel about the whole arrangement? Was she always content to be a secondary wife? The only thing that we *are* told is that the old man remained consistent to the end, quite convinced that what he was doing was right. Well, at least he had the courage to be unconventional.

Suburbages

The recent report on the decline of rural communities reiterates what this column has been saying for years. Most villages have become *suburbages*, to coin a word. They are largely commuter dormitories, to which people of many professions come home to sleep and from which they travel to work each day.

It was an inevitable development and by no means one to be deprecated. Why did villages come into existence in the first place? Because, in an age when the normal means of transport was by Shank's pony, people wanted to live near their work. And nearly all of them derived their living from the neighbouring fields. Today if the population of our villages was confined to those engaged in farming most villages would shrink to near vanishing point. So to that extent the newcomers to the villages may claim to have kept the places alive.

Nevertheless, to my mind villages need two all-important features for their continued survival. One is local industry, the other a primary school.

Until recently, planning officials have set their faces against the development of any new industries in villages, and in this they have been supported by a strong section of village opinion. That householders who have sought in a village a haven of peace and quiet should object to the establishment of a humming little factory next door is understandable but, in fact, shortsighted. For inevitably local councils are going to realize, if they have not already discovered it, that to provide piped water, sewage disposal services, refuse collection, road maintenance and all the other amenities of modern civilized life is much more expensive in sprawling villages than in compact suburbs. That being so, sooner or later they will find reasons for withdrawing first one and then probably all of these services. Several counties have already prepared plans for doing so from a large number of villages. If people choose to continue to live there, that is their affair; but from a certain date they will be on their own.

A group of thriving little businesses in a village, however, puts a different complexion on the problem. They cannot so easily be abandoned or ignored. And, after all, it was an industry which

founded the villages long ago. That industry was agriculture. In an age of mechanisation it is only natural and logical that it should be replaced by electronics factories and workshops creating other marvels of which our farming ancestors never heard or imagined.

As for primary schools, we lose them at our peril. Have you ever watched a young pet animal, say, a cat, settling into a new home? For the first few days, perhaps a week or two, the kitten remains indoors, exploring every room but dashing back indoors immediately if it is put outside. After a time it gains sufficient confidence to venture just outside into the nearer reaches of the garden. That contents it for a few more weeks. Gradually it extends its range farther and farther, into the neighbours' gardens and across the road, until, when fully adult it knows every inch of its environment within a radius of several miles (at least, in the countryside; I wouldn't know about town cats).

That is the normal sequence of events in the life of a young animal, including humans. When I was a small child my world was bounded by the rooms of our house and by the garden and farmyard attached. Then I came to know the neighbouring houses, and the village roads and fields. A neighbour's daughter took my hand when I was $4\frac{1}{2}$ years old and led me down the familiar road to the village school, a building I had often seen before. So, having become gradually acclimatised and orientated, at the age of twelve I was ready to broaden my horizons and move on to grammar school (a move, incidentally, which involved a six-mile bicycle journey each day every day, in all weathers).

But it is not natural or to my mind wise to push a five-year-old into a bus at eight o'clock in the morning and bear it off to a school, no matter how good and well appointed, ten miles away, leaving it there till half-past three, divorced from mother, home and all the familiar things of life.

All that is apart from the damage done to village life. The crowing of cocks on the farmyard dunghills, the squealing of pigs in cottage sties at mealtimes, the clanging of the blacksmith's hammer, the whinnying of horses greeting each other on their way to the fields, these are examples of the lost sounds of the countryside, and to them must now be added, in too many instances, the cries and laughter of children playing in the school playground. It is all quite sad and deplorable. I read the other day that, if Authority has its way, several thousands of village primary schools are going to be closed within the next few years. All power to the arms of parents and other villagers who rise up and oppose that appalling programme. The village school is truly an outstanding illustration of Dr. Schumacher's dictum, "Small is beautiful".

Thoughts along these lines were prompted by a visit I paid to West Devon and Cornwall. There the twentieth century has developed a little more slowly than in many other parts of Britain, so that things we tend to take for granted are there a bit of a novelty. Said one resident in a village well off the tourist track,

'When I and my family came here twelve years ago, our children were the only ones in the parish who were not born here. Now 60% of the children in the village school are newcomers. And soon there won't even be a village school.'

And he added,

'Nearly the same proportion come from one-parent families.'

He supposes that either one or the other of the partners of a broken marriage take refuge in the obscurity of a remote village or husbands who deposit their families in a rural paradise while they themselves slave all the week in London eventually find other consolations and never come back. Said my informant, with a wicked smile,

'When a couple from "up-country" takes a village cottage, the old-time villagers shake their heads and say knowingly, "Ah, they baint married, sno. Or else what do em want to come down here and hide theirselves for!".'

Village Geniuses

Visiting Mells, in the stone country of north-east Somerset, and looking at its lovely fifteenth century church I was impressed by the numerous examples of local craftsmanship it contains. For instance, the seat ends, every one different, were carved by villagers just over a hundred years ago. Most of the stained glass windows were made in the village in 1860. The eight bells, the oldest of them dating from 1716, are set to play four tunes, one of which is 'the Mells tune', composed here long ago. Near the font are two water colours of the church before its restoration in the middle of last century.

It set my mind pondering on what treasure-houses our village churches are. I admire architecture and other works of art but even more I like to think of the men and women who produced them. Having known many village geniuses in my time, it is good to realise that examples of some of their work are preserved for posterity. Of course, there are many whose skill was expressed in things so perishable or intangible that no examples can survive.

I have known expert thatchers, hedgers, sheep-shearers, gardeners, hurdle-makers and others whose work has been entirely ephemeral. I think that maybe if I had lived in a semi-literate age when work on the land offered the only scope for fulfilment to anyone born to farm work, I might have been remembered for a little while as an expert rick-maker! I served a pretty thorough apprenticeship in the ancient craft and was making good, sound ricks before I was twenty. But, of course, few ricks are now made of sheaves or loose hay or straw, so perhaps it is as well that I found something else to do.

A church cannot preserve thatch, hedges and ricks, but it is the ideal repository for such examples of old skills as are illustrated at Mells. I like, too, the memorial in the church of St. Mary Major at Ilchester, to a local man, John Wheeler Bourne, who in the middle of the nineteenth century invented a patent road-scraper. It seemed to me appropriate that the name of the man who fashioned the weathercock on St. Peter's church at Pitton, my native village, should be remembered. He was Moses Webb who, nearly two hundred years ago, had a smithy in the garden of a house where I used to live. In the chapel at Pitton are marble tablets to other worthies, including another Webb, – John, who for many years was Sunday School superintendent there. What was his claim to distinction? He was a *good* man. I remember him well.

So in a church the humble and the exalted are commemorated side by side. Mells church has as one of its greatest treasures an equestrian statue in bronze by Sir Alfred Munnings, the first horse the great artist ever sculptured. It stands on a plinth designed by Sir Edwin Lutyens, and the whole is a memorial to Edward Horner, who fell at Cambrai in 1917.

Among the incidental items I found in the booklet on Mells, copies of which are available in the church, is one about John Wesley, who preached there in September, 1785. In his *Journal* he writes:-

'Tues. 6th. I preached at Paulton and Coleford. Wed. 7th, in an open place, near the road at Mells. Just as I began, a wasp, though unprovoked, stung me upon the lip; I was afraid that it would swell, so as to hinder my speaking; but it did not. I spoke distinctly, nearly two hours in all; and was no worse for it.'

I am intrigued by the length of the sermon. To modern congregations half-an-hour seems much too long. And am reminded that at Stoke-sub-Hamdon, another church I visited not long ago, is an hourglass in an iron case (presumably another example of local craftsmanship) by the pulpit, located so that the preacher could not help seeing it.

One other thought on memorials. At Stoke-sub-Hamdon someone has had the splendid idea of planting standard roses, each with a memorial plaque, alongside the path to the church door.

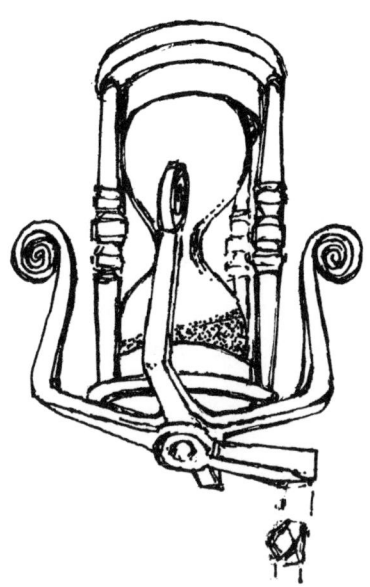

Fond Memories

'Nadderbourne?' said these two old country men. 'So that's where you comes from? I minds that place very well, eh, you?'

'I do that,' agreed the other. 'That's where we played for a fete and flower show, back fifty years ago.'

'Ah, twur a lovely day. Sweatin' hot. We sat out there in a medder at back of the old pub, – different one from what you got now – playing away for hour atter hour, and a bloke kept coming out of the pub fetching us jugs of ale. It went down well, I can tell ee. We were just about grateful to thik chap. Couple of days later, back home, we got a bill for the beer. And it come to more than what they paid us for playing the music!'

Oh dear!

Dwile-Flonking

After having been given the honour of opening Somerton's mediaeval fair in June, 1976, I expected to be away immediately after lunch, but instead stayed to enjoy the fun until the fair closed at half-past four. It was a tercentenary event, marking the three-hundredth anniversary of a charitable gift to the local schools, and mediaeval costume and sports were well to the fore. There were maypole dancing and morris dancing and some cheerful bell-ringing, but what intrigued me most was an item advertised as 'dwile flonking'.

It was new to me, so I stayed to see what it amounted to. It was mediaeval, right enough. The chaps who took part looked very much like those peasant soldiers one sees depicted in realistic pictures of the Battle of Agincourt. They were clad in sacking, tied with twine, and not much else. They joined hands and pranced around in a circle, in a manner reminiscent of ring-o'-roses, the central pivot consisting of a lad with a cloth on the end of a stick, which he dipped into a bucket of beer. As the rotating circle of dancers gathered speed, so he revolved in the opposite direction, twirling his mop, which he presently released to catch, he hoped, one of the dancers in the face. When he succeeded, he was entitled to a deep draught of beer from a cracked chamber-pot.

At least, that appeared to be the rules of the game to an uninitiated spectator, though the longer the sport went on the fewer the rules seemed to become. We stood well back. Those who were less wary got their share of sprinkled beer.

The dwile flonking occurred when the participants had already got well warmed up at the pillory. This was a contraption specially made for the occasion and probably less solid than a seventeenth century one would have been, but it served its purpose, which was to hold a prisoner fast by hands and neck while he was pelted with wet sponges. A supply was kept handy in a tub of water, and we were invited to have a go, at three sponges for fivepence.

Several public-spirited citizens volunteered to act as Aunt Sally, and reasonable order prevailed in the early stages. After a time, though, some of the youngsters grew over-excited, competing with each other to get nearer and nearer the victim till they were rubbing the sponges in his face rather than throwing them at him. The later Aunt Sallies had water squeezed down their poll and eggs squashed on their heads, till one target grew fed up with his treatment and, escaping from the pillory, began to throw sponges back at his tormentors. A lively battle ensued, and those spectators who had no wish to join in beat a hasty retreat.

It was all good, boisterous fun and probably illustrated what went on in the days of Merrie England more accurately than the modern versions of maypole and morris dancing. A couple of centuries ago, I was told, the justices of the peace would sit in judgment on sheep-stealers and other petty thieves in the stone buildings which stand by the market cross in the middle of Somerton. Judgment having been pronounced, a scaffold was erected linking that building with the pub opposite, and the offenders were strung up there and then, to dangle over the street. I'll wager there were plenty of enthusiastic spectators.

I would wager, too, that if the same spectacle were offered today and were accepted by convention, there would still be plenty of enthusiastic spectators. And plenty of people willing to pelt criminals confined in the pillory. Not with sponges, either.

Ingenuity

I eats me peas with honey,
I've done it all me life;
It makes the peas taste funny,
But it keeps 'em on me knife.

A new Innings for Outings

Written by Hilda Whitlock

As long as ever I can remember, we went for our Sunday School outing in horse-drawn vans. My fingers can still feel the texture of the furry cream coat, with the smooth, twiddly pearl buttons, that Mother insisted I should wear, in the open cart so early in the morning. Everyone assembled at the corner in the middle of Wellhouse at eight o'clock sharp, and even in June the morning air can strike chill.

I sat between Mother and Father on a wooden form placed lengthwise in the vehicle, gazing across at a row of other tots half-enveloped in the long, rough skirts of their elders. When conversation became general, I was able to twist around and peer over the side at the iron-bonded wheel spinning round so fast you could hardly see the spokes. I dangled my hand over the side and let the speeding spokes tap my fingers, till Mother spotted what was happening and turned me around with a scolding.

Our destination, Radbury Rings, about five miles away, had as its chief attraction a steep outer slope, down which we could sledge. The farmer on whose land the ancient earthwork was situated nobly provided two patient ponies to drag the sledges back to the crest, though he was humane enough to stop the boys from riding the animals uphill. Later, down at Radbury Farm, he treated us all to a strawberry tea, in the great barn. It is ungrateful of me to have forgotten his name.

I ought to be able to describe the magic of the journey home through the twilight lanes of a golden-green June evening, the air filled with the scent of honeysuckle and blundering cockchafers which bumped painfully into you like animated meteorites. Unfortunately, on the only such outing of which I really have vivid memories a steady rain came on after tea, and I travelled home crouched under a tarpaulin between my parents' knees.

With the coming of motor-buses after the first world war outing organisers became more ambitious. We now had to go to the seaside. The local carrier, Jim Day, had invested in a squarish, solidly-built Panhard which gave him half-an-hour's strenuous exercise each morning, at the starting handle. As it lived in a shed near the school playground we had an incentive to be early for school, though Miss Christian used often to come out and shepherd us to the other playground, on the far side of the school, out of earshot of the language!

Jim Day's old horse-drawn carrier's cart had had a luggage rack on top, and so did this new bus. It also lacked permanent interior seating (so that it could, on occasion, be used for transporting pigs and calves), and the passengers sat on wooden forms. That wasn't too painful on the six-mile journey to Salisbury, but the 35-mile ride to Bournemouth, bumping over rutty roads on solid tyres, was pretty excruciating. Most of the young chaps preferred to sit on the roof, their legs dangling over the side, in a manner that would now give a safety officer a fit.

I vividly recall the occasion when the outing bus stalled on a narrow hump-backed bridge about four miles on the inland side of Bournemouth. The sudden pull was too much for it; it rose gallantly to the crest and expired with a splutter. Smoke or steam poured out from under the bonnet.

Down jumped Jim Day and lifted the lid, to be enveloped in a cloud of vapour. The lads up aloft shouted encouragement. Then Jim did something, in his inexperience, which even I would now know better than to attempt. He unscrewed the radiator cap. With a bubble and a swish a jet of boiling water shot into the air like a fountain and, carried by a breeze, liberally sprinkled the gallery. The lads then had something else to shout about.

We had to fill up the radiator again and allow the engine time to cool before eventually the bus decided to start. Meantime a long queue of traffic lined up on either side of the bridge. It must have been one of the first great jams of the motor age.

At Bournemouth our headquarters were a church hall. Here we alighted and re-assembled, and here we ate our communal tea, seated, as ever, on wooden forms.

Later, we made our excursions by charabancs, and I still treasure photographs of our very bucolic-looking party, dominated by ladies with wide-brimmed straw hats, seated cheerfully in one of these open chariots, waiting for the rain to start. I believe there was a canvas hood which could be unfolded to give some protection, at least from the raindrops which descended vertically.

So far these little reminiscences have been a kind of chronicle of pilgrims' progress. We advance from cart to bus, from bus to charabanc and from charabanc to sleek, shiny modern motor-coaches. If you were to suspect, though, that we have similarly by-passed Bournemouth and now sail on to Skegness, Blackpool or Newquay you would be wrong. The Sunday School outing still goes to Bournemouth.

And there is still a Sunday School outing from Wellhouse, in spite of the fact that nearly every family now has a car. There is apparently something gay and attractive about going off on an outing with your contemporaries, especially if you are a child. You can run up and down the bus, change seats, and eat fish and chips out of newspaper. You tend to stick together on the beach, which gives you a chance of a good laugh at the queer assortment of underclothes worn by the little Mellishes and ensures that someone is on hand to rescue any of that numerous and feckless tribe in danger of being drowned. Oh yes, our Sunday School outing is still a flourishing institution. The youngsters make sure that their parents take them along.

The other day I had an invitation to another sort of outing.

'Would you like to join our Young Wives' Group on an evening outing, Hilda?'

'What? Me? A grandmother?'

'You aren't our only grandmother, by a long chalk. Most grandmothers are young nowadays. And, anyway, it's the excursion I thought might interest you. We're going to visit some excavations at an Iron Age earthwork. They're finding some interesting things, so we hear.'

'How do we get there?'

'Oh, by car. There's a spare seat in ours, if you want one. And bring a picnic supper... some sandwiches and coffee, you know. If it's fine we'll eat it up by the excavations, but if it's wet the farmer down at the bottom of the hill says we can use his big barn.'

So I accepted. And where do you think we went? To Radbury Rings.

Where are the Songsters?

Dropping in at the *Western Gazette* offices the other morning I paused on the stairs to let a busy member of the staff come striding past, two steps at a time. He was whistling. A query flashed through my mind. When did I last hear a man whistling as he went about his work? Or singing, either?

The old country proverb,

'A whistling girl and a crowing hen

Are neither good to God or men,'

would nowadays probably be written off as a bit of anti-Women's Lib. propaganda, if it meant anything at all, but are there whistling girls still?

When I was a boy I often used to hear my mother singing as she went about her housework. And out in the fields a ploughman whistling as he followed his horses along the furrow was one of the familiar sounds of the countryside. It is true that my mother was no prima donna. My father occasionally used to earn a sharp retort when he commented,

'Well, if anybody wouldn't come out of a fire to hear that he'd deserve to stay there and be burned!'

My mother would look puzzled at first, until she realized what he was talking about. She hadn't realized she had been singing. The sounds just came naturally.

I know how she felt. My own efforts are decidedly *sotto voce*, but from time to time I find myself whistling or singing very softly to myself. Or humming. I do it unconsciously. My wife remarks,

'Why on earth do you try to hum while you're eating cake?'

I had no idea I was doing so. My mind was elsewhere.

Or sometimes she exclaims,

'If you must hum, let's have a change from that dreary old tune.'

'What dreary old tune?' I ask, in surprise.

'Well, I think it was supposed to be "Onward, Christian soldiers".'

She may be right, I wouldn't know. And that, of course, is the secret of singing or whistling to yourself. You do it spontaneously, without thinking. So why don't we sing or whistle any more?

The more you think about it, the more curious it becomes. Consider how popular music is today. Fortunes are spent by the public on pop records and other records. Almost any teenager could reel off the list of records on the Top of the Pops. But why, then, don't they sing them? When I was a teenager and such songs as 'Yes, we have no Bananas' and 'We want a Little White Room' were popular, we used to walk down the lane, singing them. Just as my father used to chant the songs of his youth, such as 'For me, for me, She's waiting there for me,' from the top of the corn-rick he was making. As for hymns, we knew four or five entire hymn-books by heart. Perhaps today's teenagers could likewise sing or whistle the tunes that are found at the top of the charts, though there is little evidence of it.

Perhaps it is because we have become self-critical. When my wife is busy in the kitchen she usually has the radio turned on. So did my son when he was tractor-driving in the fields, before he emigrated to Canada. My mother and father couldn't do that. If they wanted music, they had to make it themselves. Nowadays we might argue that the sounds produced by our radio or record-player are of much higher quality, musically, than those emanating from our own larynx. So let us remain silent in the presence of the experts.

If that is the explanation, it is on a par with the present predilection for spectator sports. Is the man who prefers to listen to Harry Secombe the same chap who prefers to watch cricket or football rather than play it? It could be, though I do not find the argument completely satisfying. For making other kinds of music is not on the decline. Pop groups, bands and music-makers of all kind abound. There are as many amateur musicians around as ever there were. It is just that they don't sing or whistle at their work any more. I wonder why?

Shopping for Mother!

A talk I gave to the Yeovil Retired Townsmen's Guild prompted a lot of memories, including one by a member who lived near Dorchester in his youth. He recalled how the village carrier, who trundled into Dorchester about twice a week in his tilt-covered cart, used to get entrusted with a remarkable variety of errands. One was to buy ladies' hats! Several of the village housewives used to trust him to buy their headgear, having given him instructions about what sort of hat they wanted. How did he manage about size?

'Oh, I tries 'em on,' he said. 'I do know roughly how big their heads be.'

He patronised the same milliner's, year after year, so the proprietor got a very good idea of what her customers liked; and it was always possible to change any unsuitable ones in the following week.

I remember that in the days when my father used to go to market in pony and trap he often took notes to the drapers for Mother. Later in the day he would pick up brown-paper parcels of what, I think, were underwear.

A Homington (Salisbury) reader suggests that the dialect expression, 'sno', (beloved by Jonas, of Cowleaze Farm, years ago) was confined to Wiltshire and not used in other Wessex shires. I tried this theory on my Yeovil audience, to have it immediately refuted. It was, and is, used just as freely in Somerset and Dorset, they assured me. 'Sno', incidentally, is simply an abbreviation of 'dost thee know'. .

The Flying Rabbit

'Yur! I got to be busy fer a minute or two,' said the farmer, in the tactful way that countrymen have. 'Thee go and talk to thik ole veller over there. He'll tell thee some yarns.'

It was in a farmyard in West Dorset, and the 'ole veller' indicated was an insignificant little chap who had been sorting potatoes in the barn and was now sitting on a hay bale, munching at a lunch of bread and cheese. His tattered old raincoat was tied around the middle by a length of binder-twine, his whiskers grew like goose's down right down his neck, and, as he ate, his Adam's apple jerked strenuously up and down, like a wild animal trying to escape from a trap.

After one or two false starts we finally got into conversation on the subject of rats, and from then on we ranged over all the animals of the countryside and the ways and means of compassing their destruction. I learned quite a lot. Presently he paused, with his lamb's-foot pocket-knife halfway through a hunk of cheese which he held against a dark-stained thumb and fixed me with a bleary eye.

'I've a-done a thing what have never before been done by man!' he announced dramatically.

This sounded interesting, and I knew I had only to wait to hear what the unique feat was.

'Twur one Sat'day afternoon, along this time of the year,' he went on, deftly finishing his operation on the cheese and popping it into his mouth, where it seemed to make no difference to his flow of language. 'I wur out wi' the dogs, sno, and wur coming along be ... ah well, never thee mind where twur! ... twur down nigh the river, anyhow. Bimeby old Gyp – that wur one of the dogs I had along that time – ah, knowin' old bitch she wur – smell a keeper half a mile off – one of the baist dogs I ever had ... well, she put up this yer rabbit out from under a bramble, see, and he went skedaddling all along be the bank of the river, and I ups with me gun to shoot en, but tother dog, see ... he wur a youngster, sno, and didn't know no better ... he took atter the rabbit and var near catched en. Not that he had an icicle's chance in a frying-pan of ever catching the darn thing ... you knows how rabbits da dodge

... but he stopped I vrum getting a shot, sno. Aye, I wur afraid I should hit the dog. I stood there wi' me gun bar'l a-wobbling up and down, and then the rabbit went up a tree!

'Aye, he did, sno. One of the sem yer willow trees, along be the riverside. They be often holler, sno ... you knows that ... and rabbits do lie up in em reg'lar sometimes. Well, up goes the rabbit, up this yer holler tree ... and up goes the dog atter en. Twur one of these yer slanting trees, lack, ... so there wadn' nothing special about that.

'Well, there wur the dog half-way up, yowping away as though he'd set down on a hot stove and slithering about cos he'd just seed how far the ground were below en, and there wur the rabbit, right up the top, where the tree had bin pollarded, croopying about among the little twigs. Ah, I could see thik rabbit var' well, and I could ha' knocked en flying there and then. An' then I stopped, and I says to meself, Albert! Bide thee a minute, and theet'll do summat what no man have ever done avore.

'Aye, that's what I said to meself, and that's what I done. I could see, sno, that thik there rabbit were reckoning that he wur in no very safe place up thik tree, wi' thik 'ar dog a-hollering in his yur-ole, ... and, sure 'nough, in about half-a-minute he took off... aye, right off the top of the stub, auver into the medder. And that's when I shot en. Right in mid-air, as you mid say. I scat he properly, and when he hit the ground he wur as daid's a door-nail!'

The old man paused to take another bite of bread and cheese, and just then the farmer came back so I left him to finish his lunch in peace. A contented man! He had done something that no other man had ever done! He had shot a rabbit flying!

Coincidences

Everybody can recall from their life's experiences at least one or two coincidences, but two happened to me on the same day during a week-end at Plymouth. On the Saturday afternoon we played truant from a congress we were attending and instead went shopping in the city's splendid shopping precinct. And there, in one of the big stores, we ran into some neighbours from our own village. They had come on a coach trip organised by

Ilchester Women's Institute. It was ages since we had last visited Plymouth, and ages since the W.I. had organised such an excursion, and neither party knew what the other was planning. So we all had a surprise, meeting so unexpectedly about ninety miles from home.

But the other coincidence was much more remarkable. In the hotel lounge late in the evening we got into conversation with some Australian, American and Canadian tourists who had arrived by coach that afternoon. This was their farthest west point of a fortnight's tour that had taken them from London to Scotland and back through the Lake District and the Midlands to Bath and the West Country. So we exchanged notes, and one of the Canadians said he came from Winnipeg. I said that I had visited Winnipeg several times and was indeed expecting to go to Canada again in the near future, though not to Winnipeg this time. We are planning to visit our son and his family on Vancouver Island. One thing led to another, as it does, and the Canadian was in due course supplied with the information that our son went to work in Canada and married a Canadian girl.

'Where did that happen?' he asked.

'Oh, at a little place you never heard of, I expect,' I told him. 'A tiny little township called Waskada, about 250 miles west of Winnipeg, on the Manitoba/Saskatchewan border.'

Whereupon, with a broad grin, he dived for his wallet, brought out a sort of identity card which apparently Canadians carry, and pointed out the name of his birth-place, there recorded. Waskada, Manitoba! He had left there when he was ten but knew some of the families whom we have met when visiting our son.

The chances of such an encounter in England between two strangers who had ever heard of, let alone visited, such a small and remote place must be several million to one.

Martock Beans

A colleague drew my attention to the concluding paragraph of a feature article in *The Times*. A writer who was setting up house in Norfolk mentioned that he had been promised 'a packet of Martock beans, as grown in the ancient parish since the thirteenth century'. Looking like wrinkled black marbles, they are a strain peculiar to the West Country and come complete with the legend on the packet: 'If you do shake a Martock man, you do hear the beans rattle.'

Queried my colleague, 'Do you know anything about this?' No, I didn't, so I made it my business to find out.

My first emissary went into a store in Martock and enquired innocently, 'Did they know what Martock beans were, and where could a friend get a packet?'

'They just fell about laughing,' she told me.

'We be Martock beans,' they said. 'All Martock folk born and bred be Martock beans.'

Another old friend who lives at Martock added further information.

'In the old days,' he told me, 'Martock men had a great reputation for hard drinking. Their capacity was said to be even greater than that of the men of Middlezoy, which is saying a lot. At harvest-time, every morning when the harvesters went out with their reap-hooks to cut the corn they were given a two-gallon cask of cider, which had to last them till breakfast-time. They were also given five handfuls of black beans, which they put inside their shirts. Their belts, of course, prevented the beans from slipping down and falling out of their trouser legs. That is why it was standard practice, in the old days, though not if you wanted to avoid a row, to ask a Martock man, How many beans make five?

'Well, the purpose of the beans was to keep the harvesters sober enough to stand on their feet. As they got through those two gallons of cider they would, between swigs, eat handfuls of beans, which counteracted, to some extent, the effects of the drink. So now you can see why, if you do shake a Martock man you do hear the beans rattle!'

'I can indeed,' I agreed. 'But this bit about the little black beans like wrinkled marbles, is that a leg-pull?'

'No, I wouldn't say that. The beans were obviously field beans, or tic beans. You can buy these nowadays from merchants, but in the old days farmers would keep their own seed and use it for year after year, generation after generation, century after century. There may well be beans on farms around Martock that have grown there for hundreds of years, long enough to have become a special strain.'

My enquiries produced several incidental items of information. I was asked whether I knew what a 'Crewkerne chap' was. Answer. A thistle – which sounds somewhat derogatory to Crewkerne.

Did I know what being 'stabbed by a Bridport dagger' meant? I did, having been caught out by that on a BBC quiz once. It means 'to be hanged', a Bridport dagger being a rope, for the making of which Bridport used to be famous.

Following this note, the vicar of Martock, Rev. Peter Coney, sent me a packet of genuine Martock beans, with his good wishes, commenting that 'they have been grown on at least one farm for time out of mind. The earliest reference to them is in the manorial account rolls of 1293–4. I obtained a supply from the farmer and normally part with them in return for donations to the church restoration appeal.'

In due course I committed them to the soil and later took a harvest. They were undistinguished field beans, like small, brownish-black marbles, and could not compare with modern varieties.

Mr. Coney tells me that Martock has another claim to fame. In 1226 tithes were being paid to the rector on hay, pork, silver, cows, wool, lambs, cheese and 'eggs at Easter'. This is apparently the earliest literary reference to Easter eggs!

When writing of Martock beans I also mentioned 'Crewkerne chaps', alias thistles. This prompted the information that a whole group of villages along the Somerset-Dorset borders have local nicknames. Hardington people are traditionally known as 'Hardington Peewits'; Hazelbury Plucknett folk as 'Hazelbury Lions'; the people of North Perrot as 'North Perrot Monkeys'. There are a number of others, which my informants could not remember.

Casting my mind over the villages in other parts of Wessex that I know well, I could not think of any similar group of nicknames, except that the people of Aldbourne, near Marlborough, are known as 'Aldbourne dabchicks' and a story is told which purports to account for the epithet. Elsewhere the only one I had heard concerns Rampisham, in Dorset, whose inhabitants have, at times, been called 'Rampisham sinners'. The fact that Rampisham is pronounced locally as 'Ransom' may have something to do with it. In fact, a local tale which used to be often repeated recounted how the Rampisham church choir once paid an official visit, on a festival day of some sort, to the neighbouring

church of Evershot. As they entered the church they were met by
the strains of an anthem sung by the Evershot choir,

'The day of Jubilee is come,
    Return, ye Ransomed sinners, home.'

Whereupon the Rampisham choir turned round and went
home in high dudgeon, complaining that 'they didn't see why
Rampisham sinners were any worse than Evershot ones.' But I
am sure the story is apocryphal.

The Aldbourne dabchick, incidentally, is explained by the
story of how a dabchick was once seen on the pond in the
otherwise waterless village of Aldbourne. The villagers were so
puzzled by this strange bird that they sent for the oldest
inhabitant, who asked to be wheeled three times round the pond
in a wheelbarrow, so that he could get a good look at the visitor.
He then pronounced that it was a dabchick. To the residents of
Ramsbury, who had an ancient feud with Aldbourne, the term
'Aldbourne dabchick' was a useful epithet of opprobrium. The
Ramsbury boys would follow the Aldbourne carrier's cart
shouting, 'Yar! Aldbourne dabchicks! Yah! Aldbourne dabchicks!'

Village nicknames are a subject introduced by the mention of
Martock Beans. I invited other examples.

A Long Sutton reader contributed:

'High Ham Lads; Low Ham Men; Pitney Pigs; Upton Bobbies;
Sutton Bulldogs; Long Load Lankets; Martock Beans.

But in a Langport version some of the terms were different. My
correspondent told me he learned the following rhyme when he
was a boy, seventy years ago, from an old man then in his
seventies: -

High Ham Lassies; Low Ham Lads;
Pitney Pigs, and Aller Scabs;
Langport Bulldogs; Somerton Hounds;
Martock Beans and Sutton Clowns.'

The Langport version, it will be noted, is quite complimentary
to Langport but not to Long Sutton, whereas in the Long Sutton
version the village has appropriated the Bulldogs for itself!

My Long Sutton contributor also remembered an uncomplimentary rhyme he learned as a child about the small
neighbouring village of Knole.

'Old Knole, you dirty old hole,
    Without any church or steeple,

A heap of mud at everybody's door,
Old Knole, you dirty old hole.'
Children loved to chant such insulting verses to youngsters from the villages in question.

A Lymington (Hampshire) reader who was brought up at Stoke-sub-Hamdon, near Yeovil, remembers that in the early years of this century she knew the Stoke people as 'Stokies'; the people of Montacute as 'Monacks'; and the inhabitants of Odcombe as 'Odcombe Squats'. One can guess at how 'Stokies' and 'Monacks' were derived, both nicknames representing a juggling with the village names. It sounds as though Odcombe were settled by squatters, which is likely enough, I would think.

It is rather intriguing, though, that all these nicknames belonged to a smallish area in south and central Somerset and just over the border in Dorset. None from any other part of Wessex. I wonder why?

Guidance

This is the true story of an event that occurred at Exmouth just over a hundred years ago. At that time if you wanted to go from Exmouth to Exeter you crossed the estuary of the Exe by ferryboat and caught the Exeter train at Starcross station.

A young man staying at Exmouth woke up in the middle of the night possessed by an overwhelming conviction that he had to go down to the ferry. Reluctantly he got up, dressed and walked down to the shore, convinced that no ferryboat would be there. The ferryman lived at Starcross, on the other side of the estuary, and was doubtless asleep in bed.

He was surprised, therefore, to find the ferryboat waiting for him. The ferryman said that someone had hailed him, shouting out of the night, and told him there was a passenger waiting on the other side. No-one else was in sight, so the young man, still acting on a strong impulse, decided to go across. He was just in time to catch a night train to Exeter.

There his 'guidance' abandoned him, and he wandered about the street till daylight, cursing himself for being a fool. Cold and hungry, he slipped into a hotel for breakfast. The waiter, chatting, mentioned that the Assizes were being held that day, so, having nothing better to do, he decided to look in, to see if anything interesting was happening.

It was a murder case. The defendant was a carpenter, whose defence was an alibi. At the time of the murder, he said, he was working on some windows at a gentleman's house miles away. Could he prove that? Well, no, the gentleman's family had been away. So ... no alibi. If only, said the carpenter, I could find that man who came up and talked with me while I was working. He was a friend of the householder and stayed for a chat when he found there was nobody at home. He borrowed a pencil to make a note in his pocket-book. But, lamented the carpenter, I don't know who he was or where he lived.

Whereupon the young man, deeply moved, asked to be allowed to give evidence. He was the visitor that day, he said, and as corroboration produced his pocket-book in which was the note made with the carpenter's pencil.

Only his evidence could have secured the carpenter's acquittal. He remained always convinced that the guidance he received was supernatural, nor is it easy to think of any alternative explanation. It must have been a decidedly powerful influence to get both him and the ferryman out of bed in the middle of the night.

The Village Retreats on Itself

Travelling across country between Yeovil and Bournemouth on
November 5th, 1975, and back by a different route the next day, I
failed to see a single bonfire or the embers of one. No doubt if I
could have peeped into private back gardens I would have found
a few, but the communal or village bonfires seem to be a thing of
the past. When I was a boy we always had a huge one on a hill
overlooking the village and spent every evening and Saturday
afternoon for the previous fortnight collecting wood and bushes
for it. Most of the village assembled there about six o'clock on
Bonfire Night, and as the fire died down the older, the more
decorous and the small children trotted home, leaving the more
boisterous spirits to carry on the revels till a late hour. The things
we did with gunpowder and carbide tins, to say nothing of squibs
in oil-drums, would have horrified those right-minded people
who nowadays are disturbed by the dangers of ordinary
fireworks.

The reasons for the change are complex, but some of them
became quite clear to me the other day when I revisited a village
which I used to know well but had not seen for several years. I
have, in fact, a picture of that village taken about the turn of the
century, and it provokes comment for its neatness and tidiness.
The cottage gardens are all neatly planted with rows of
vegetables, the elm and willow trees are all pollarded, the hedges
are laid and trimmed, the houses and barns have patches of new,
bright-yellow thatch, and the atmosphere is one of well-ordered
industry – so well-ordered that the place looks bare. Now it gives
the impression of a secretive, over-grown place. The gardens are
planted not with vegetables but with flowers and, more
particularly, with shrubs and ornamental trees, in many
instances protected by fairly high board fences. Shrubs and trees,
like the surviving hedges, have been allowed to grow unchecked,
so that, with a few exceptions, each house is buried in a nest of
greenery. The development is deliberate, and the houses must be
pleasant and private places to live in. But the point is that the
residents prefer things that way. Neighbours, they feel, may be all
very well, but it's nice to be able to shut them out.

When one had been working all day alone in the fields, it was pleasant to be able to chat with a neighbour over the garden hedge, as one straightened one's back from weeding cabbages. But when one has spent the day commuting in a crowded train or bus to a crowded town, by evening one has seen enough of the human race. Our excessively large population is breeding its own reaction, which in some instances takes the form of withdrawal from social life and in others, especially among young people, in vandalism and other anti-social behaviour. And it's really nothing to wonder at, though the effects may not be to our liking.

When the influx of newcomers was beginning in one of the villages I knew well, one of the immigrants, a retired chap, soon became involved in a dispute with his neighbour – over an alleged encroachment over about two feet into his garden. This was at a time when land was cheap and in plentiful supply, and used as I was to thinking in acres, to squabble over two feet seemed to me to be petty. So, as I had plenty of land just down the road and as this poor chap was rather restricted in the matter of garden space, I invited him to help himself to as much as he wanted. He looked at me as though I was mad and hardly spoke to me for weeks afterwards. He didn't want more space; he wanted to show his authority over his own little patch. I had spoiled his little exercise in kingmanship.

ALL KINDS OF PLANTS

A Corner of My Garden

A corner of my garden which gives me immense quiet pleasure owes nothing to any art, design or even labour of mine. Beneath the lilacs is a thicket of small brushwood, springing up from the lilac roots among the moss-grown paving-stones. The moss here is thick and green and forms a perfect backcloth to the companies of snowdrops which, now in early February, stand there motionless. Pure white snowdrops, bright green moss and grey stones, all in a peaceful corner of an English garden are a sight to make even an English winter seem worthwhile.

Memories of Apples

The Devil never keeps his bargains. Many years ago he struck one with a Devonshire brewer named Frankan, who, it is said, was alarmed at the effect the new cult of cider-drinking was having on his trade. So he sold his soul to the Devil in return for frosts on May 19th, 20th and 21st sufficiently hard to ruin the apple-blossom. In recent years the Devil has been observing his side of the contract only half-heartedly; in 1978 and again in 1980 he ignored it entirely.

Everywhere the trees were loaded, with branches splitting under the weight of fruit. The gales of early September littered the ground beneath the trees with fallen fruit, yet the crop left on the trees still seemed undiminished.

A traveller can estimate his distance from London by observing the hand-painted advertisements for apples at roadside farmsteads and gardens. Near the capital the posters advertise 'WINDFALL APPLES' at so much per pound. Farther out, the captions change to 'WINDFALLS' or, more often, 'FALLERS'. But when he sees a sign saying simply 'MORGAN SWEETS', he knows he is in the West Country. Who, apart from a West Countryman, would know that Morgan Sweet is an apple?

A neighbour gave me a bag of Tom Putts. As I stuffed my nose into the bag and breathed in deeply the lovely aromatic fragrance brought back memories of earliest childhood. A Tom Putt tree then stood in our garden. It had to be cut down to make way for an extension to the house which my father made in 1922, but I had time to grow familiar with the beautiful red fruit before that disaster. Many a time I was bidden to 'go out and pick up the Tom Putts' – always 'the Tom Putts'; never 'the apples'.

The old West Country wassailing song refers, in most of its versions, to apples being stored in 'a little heap under the stairs', and that indeed was, and probably still is, a favourite store-place. It always was in our house, but the cupboard under the stairs was not nearly adequate for all our apples. They overflowed everywhere, notably into the bedrooms. In October and November my brother and I used to have to pick our way along a narrow path between heaps of apples from the bedroom door to the bed. The best specimens, and the William pears, were set out on the broad windowsill. What a pleasant, soporific atmosphere for the last moments of a busy day!

When my wife said, 'Now where shall we put these Tom Putts?' I knew there was only one place. On the windowsill of my study. Whenever I raise my head from my typewriter they beam at me, appetisingly red in the sunlight. 'They'll attract the wasps,' warned my wife, but it was a risk I was prepared to take. It is worth a wasp or two to have all the fragrance of an autumn orchard trapped in one's workroom.

Incidentally, the Tom Putt is a real West Country apple. It derives its name from its originator, the Rev. Tom Putt, who was vicar of Trent, near Sherborne, long ago. I thought that the variety had become obsolete and had survived only in long-mature trees here and there in the West Country, so I was delighted the other day to see it listed in a contemporary catalogue. It is still possible to buy a young Tom Putt tree.

What an enviable memorial – to be remembered as the originator of a favourite apple! Some men achieve fame through fighting wars, or negotiating peace treaties, or inventing machines to perform miracles, or painting pictures, or composing symphonies, or even writing books, and their achievements are recorded for posterity to read in history books. But if old Tom Putt knows what is going on down here in this muddly world, how happy he must be when he hears good country folk, descendants of those he used to minister to, say 'Ah, we must go out in the orchard now and pick up them Tom Putts.'

After writing the above I was introduced to another old West Country variety of apple – Nurdle-top, or perhaps it should be written 'Knurdle-top'. The name is apparently descriptive, for the top end of the apple is pinched and puckered, and at the back of my mind I seem to remember that there is a dialect word, 'knurdle', meaning just that. Do any readers know it? This apple is not much to look at, being green and rather pointed, but it is good for both eating and cooking.

A Henstridge reader sent me an apple which seemed to her to match my description of a 'Nurdle-top', and it is indeed identical with the one I have. A Queen Camel reader phoned to say that the local name of this variety is 'Stubbard'. Other old-time varieties still known in these parts are 'Beauty of Kent' and 'Bell'.

A Shaftesbury reader who retired some years ago from

Alderbury, near Salisbury, brought with him from his old garden a cordon apple of a variety which he had always known as 'Churchwarden'. He is now convinced that it is a 'Morgan Sweet'. He remembers another useful cooking variety he had in the same orchard; everyone called it a 'Beefing', but he now thinks the original name was 'Beaufin'.

Then there was the 'Caraway Russet', which has a crescent-shaped scab or scar on every apple. And also the 'Court Pendu Plat', which has been described as the oldest variety in cultivation, possibly originating with the Romans. My Shaftesbury correspondent has one that is still quite small though over twenty years old, it grows so slowly.

A Crewkerne reader queried the origin of the variety Tom Putt. He said that its breeder was a Thomas Putt, better known as Black Tom, who was the son of a rector of Gittisham, near Honiton, and a member of a well-known Devonshire family. Professor W. G. Hoskins, who knows Devon intimately, makes the same statement, attributing the apple to 'Thomas Putt (1722–1787), a barrister, who perfected it and who planted the Beech Walk on Gittisham Hill'. But Dorset people will have none of this, and a reader who was born in Trent, where the other Thomas Putt was vicar, assures me that a big old apple tree, descendant of one planted by Tom Putt, still grows there.

A Gardening Year

Feeling, as a retired farmer, the urge to grow something, I took up gardening. In one respect I was on familiar ground, for, when farming, I had from time to time grown horticultural crops, such as cabbages, cauliflower, swedes and potatoes. In another, it was an entirely novel experience, for it is well known that a farmer leaves his gardening to God. Seasonal work in the garden always coincides with the busy time on the farm, and, of course, the farm has priority. With no farm to distract me, for the first time in my life I was able to tackle garden work at the proper time ... well, more or less.

Farming made me regard things from a utilitarian point of view, so, although I grew some flowers to keep my wife happy, I concentrated on vegetables. I was, however, ambitious. I wanted to try something new. So in the winter I ploughed methodically through seed catalogues and ordered a selection of almost everything on offer, particularly the unusual vegetables.

I fortunately have a garden with good soil. Although overlying a heavy clay sub-soil, it has been cultivated as a kitchen garden for hundreds of years and so has a good friable texture, and ample supplies of farmyard manure are available from the adjacent farm. So I had a splendid start.

Shall I recount my mistakes first? One that I made could have been predicted for a farmer-turned-gardener. I overestimated the amount of seed I needed. I cheerfully sowed line after line of brassicas – cabbages, savoys, broccoli, purple-sprouting broccoli, kale, cauliflower – as though I had a whole field in which to transplant them. And when the time came to transplant, I had used up most of the available ground.

I compromised, by leaving many of the plants where they were, after thinning them. The treatment worked quite well with some varieties, notably kale and purple-sprouting, but not with brussels sprouts. Sprouts and cabbages seem to need transplanting, in spite of the check it gives them. Is it because they are placed deeper in the soil?

The same miscalculation induced me to grow more than I needed of beetroot, parsnips, swedes, seakale, beet, and, at certain seasons, lettuces. I ought to have allowed myself more space for a succession of peas, dwarf beans and carrots.

The weeding in June and July almost defeated me. Hand-weeding onions is a particularly tedious job, but I understand that there is now an effective chemical, Alicep, available for pre-emergent application. I shall have to do something too, about carrot fly, which attacked most of the main crop of carrots.

A mistake I made in ignorance concerns a salad crop I had never before seen growing – endive. Sold in April, this produced strong plants like curly-leaved lettuce, by the end of May. For some inexplicable reason, I had the idea that one let them grow all the summer, cut them down in autumn, and then blanched the shoots in winter. Not so. The thing to do is to put big flower-pots, boxes or some other covering over them as soon as they are large enough, blanching them where they grow. I did not realise this until the first ones were shooting up the flower stems. With the later plants I had good success.

Winter blanching is the treatment accorded to chicory – at least, to the standard Witloof variety. My crop was remarkably satisfactory. The plants grew a mass of leaves, a foot or two tall, and I was able to use some of the early ones for cooking as spinach. By autumn the roots were as big as large parsnips. I then lifted them in batches, cut off the leaves and planted them upright in barrels and boxes, with enough soil to cover the crowns by about three inches. I found, in fact, that garden peat was better than ordinary soil. As the weather was mild, I was able to leave the roots in the ground until each new batch was needed and so had a succession of excellent chicory shoots all the winter, when, as I delighted to point out to my wife, the stuff was selling in the shops at exorbitant prices.

The other two varieties of chicory are used in different ways. Red Verona, according to the text-books, should be treated in the same way as Witloof, but I found that the shoots it produced were rather frail and spindly. However, I had to leave most of the roots in the ground for lack of barrel space, and during the autumn and winter these produced nice compact heads that looked like red lettuces and had a similar taste. They made a striking contribution to the winter salad bowl. Of course, the winter was exceptionally mild, and I think that in a normal season they could probably benefit from a covering of dung or straw.

Sugar loaf chicory is an autumn and winter substitute for lettuce, being very like a Cos lettuce with a solid heart, the leaves are crisp, but rather tough, and only the inner ones are worth using. I did not attempt to force or blanch this variety but just took what offered.

The Chinese cabbage, or Pe-Tsai, also resembles a Cos lettuce in appearance but has thick white mid-ribs to its leaves. It can be eaten as a salad or cooked like ordinary cabbage, or the mid-ribs can be stripped and cooked separately, like seakale beet or asparagus. It is a pleasant and unusual vegetable but with no very distinctive flavour. I obeyed instructions not to sow before July, which was just as well, for the seeds germinate and grow with remarkable speed. The heads are at their best for a week or two, after which they quickly send up flower-heads.

By way of contrast, one of the slowest-growing plants I experimented with was the American Cress, or Land Cress. It looks and tastes like watercress, but is slow to start (I nearly dug up the plot and sowed it with some other crop) and slower still to grow. The flavour is rather stronger than that of watercress, so one does need less of it in a salad. I have left mine in ground over winter, to produce a second crop in spring.

I grew several herbs besides. One was Fennel, which produces a feathery foliage which my wife finds quite attractive in flower arrangements, but which is normally grown for use in fish sauces. However, it can be eaten with other salads and tastes strongly of aniseed. So does Dill, which closely resembles it. My Fennel plot stood the winter and produced a strong new growth of leaves in Spring, and I am told that I shall now have it forever. The Dill, on the other hand, lasted for about a month and then died down. We used both Fennel and Dill sparingly in salads.

Two other short-lived herbs grown for salad were Chervil and Rocket. Both ran up to flower very quickly and then were finished. I liked the Chervil but found the Rocket rather insipid. My Basil seed failed to germinate, and I am told that this often happens. Borage, on the other hand, grew quickly and produced a thicket of strong plants, which later yielded a prolific harvest of bright blue flowers beloved of bees.

'You must be expecting to drink a lot of claret cup,' commented a visitor, that being one of the best known uses of Borage, but I grew it for salad. Some gardeners say it tastes like cucumber. I cannot endorse that but it certainly has a distinctive flavour which I find pleasant. One should use the youngest leaves on which the bristly hairs have not become too strong.

Naturally in the corner of my garden devoted to herbs I have those perennials – Thyme, Sage, Mint and Rosemary – besides which I grew Marjoram and Parsley for flavouring. I also sowed a packet of Summer Savory, of which practically every seed grew, producing a couple of ranks of a branching, tiny leaved plant which reminds me, in appearance, of the Kochia or burning-bush. We used the leaves both fresh and dried as flavouring, particularly for beans and peas. At first I could not identify the flavour; then I realised that it was producing a hot taste in the mouth very like pepper. I imagine it could well be used as a substitute for pepper.

A salad plant which I grew with success but did not greatly care for is Corn Salad. It is a little plant of lowly growth, from which one can take pickings of leaves in autumn and again in spring. Some may like it, but I don't; it has, to my mind, a rather sickly flavour.

On a border under a sunny stone wall I deposited in spring a cartload of farmyard manure and planted in it the seeds of marrows, courgettes and pumpkins. And naturally they grew fast and produced prolifically, so that I did not need to employ the old gardener's trick of feeding the fruits with sugar-water. At least, the courgettes and marrows did; the pumpkins I reduced to one fruit per plant, as I had ambitions to win a prize at a pumpkin show.

By September my biggest pumpkin seemed fully grown, so I cut it, rolled it on to a sack, and with the aid of a neighbour, lifted it into a wheelbarrow. It weighed 90lb. Unfortunately, I picked the wrong show. At one show, I believe it was Ansty in Wiltshire, I read in the *Western Gazette* that the winning pumpkin weighed only 45lb. but at the show I chose, which was the Broughton Pumpkin Show in Hampshire, my 90lb. monster didn't even get a mention. I believe the winner weighed something over 130lb.

There was some debate about what to do with it. Well-grown pumpkins are excellent vegetables, their yellow flesh providing an appetizing ingredient for either a savoury or sweet dish, but ninety pounds of pumpkin is quite a challenge. Eventually I took it to a Harvest Home supper, which was being held to raise funds for a Church heating scheme. We cut it into slices and auctioned them. The pumpkin produced £6.50 – a highly gratifying figure in 1975.

The courgettes, by the way, needed to be cut as soon as they were about six inches long, in order to stimulate the plant to keep on producing fruit. I liked the Zucchini variety, which produced a lovely golden courgette which seemed to us to have a more delicate flavour than the others.

Three root vegetables with which I had considerable success were Salsify, Scorzonera and Hamburg Parsley. I have no particular recommendations for growing them. I sowed them in rows, like parsnips, and kept them reasonably free from weeds. A deep soil is needed however, or the roots will be badly forked. All are used in winter and kept in ground until required, except in a very severe season. They are cooked like parsnips, though salsify in particular can be cut into slices and fried after the initial boiling. All are delicacies and make good eating. My wife does not like scorzonera, as it has to be boiled and then peeled whiled hot and cooked again.

In spring I read in an old encyclopedia that the shoots of salsify could be cut when they were about six to twelve inches high and cooked like asparagus. We tried this, although they ended by being cooked very much like cabbage, though not too long, certainly less than half an hour. They were delicious – one of the nicest vegetables I have ever tasted.

I grew some of the self-blanching celery for salad, but got it in too late and so had only stunted plants. It seemed satisfactory but does not produce succulent sticks as ordinary celery. From its name I imagine that a new item in the catalogue, called Celtuce, might be a lettuce with a celery flavour but it proved to be a kind of lettuce of which one ate the pith from the centre of the tall thick stem. Not very exciting, though it is easy to grow. Seakale beet and spinach beet are not exactly novelties to me, but we like them both as second vegetables, particularly the thick white stems of seakale beet. Again both are easy to grow. I have also tried a golden variety of beetroot instead of the usual red one, but when cooked it looks colourless and less appetizing.

In autumn I sowed some of a specially recommended winter-hardy lettuce, named Valdor, and was pleased with how well it stood the winter, being ready for transplanting in late February. I also had some of those new Japanese onions which are supposed to continue growing all through the winter and to produce good bulbs in June, when last year's crop has been used up.

On the whole, my first season as an amateur gardener, proved more successful than I could have hoped, and I went into the second year with enthusiasm unabated.

Last year an Ottawa (Canada) reader, drew my attention to the odd and somewhat neglected subject of companion planting. Old-time gardeners used to know something about this. They would, for example, never sow onions near beans and peas, or cabbages near a strawberry bed. Cabbages were best planted near beans and peas, and onions sown in alternate rows with carrots. Knowledgeable gardeners sometimes planted cuttings of mint or a lavender bush at the end of a cabbage row. Parsley was grown among rose bushes. Gardeners with Continental experience would plant a few garlic crowns in their rose beds; they claimed that would 'Bring out the scent' of the roses.

Most gardeners of the old school could give no reasons for these principles behind their planting programmes. All they knew was that beans 'Didn't do' when grown next to onions, and that horse-radish 'helped' potatoes. Current research, however, indicates that their observations were, on the whole, sound.

There is nothing magical about the compatibility or incompati ility of plants. Apart from the unwisdom of planting two species of plants greedy for nitrogen, for instance, near each other in soils with limited supplies of nitrogen, the basic fact is that certain plants produce, usually in their roots, chemical substances which are deleterious to certain others, while others produce substances which other species find beneficial.

A plant which was the subject of early experiments was Wormwood (*Artemisia*), from which a toxic substance, Absinthin, was isolated. Present in both roots and leaves it spreads into the soil around the plant. As a result, very few plants will thrive near Wormwood. Extracts of Wormwood can also be used for infusions to repel slugs, flea-beatles and other garden pests. Another garden plant which has a similar stunting effect on many plants grown near it is Fennel. It seems to be particularly incompatible with tomatoes.

Most aromatic herbs produce fairly concentrated chemicals, most of which, however, are beneficial to plants of other species and some of which repel insect pests. Sage, Mint and Lavender, are said to repel cabbage butterflies, and Sage grown nearby is said to improve the quality of cabbages. Dill aids the growth of cabbages and lettuce but suppresses that of carrots. Parsley is a good companion of both tomatoes and roses. Ants, aphids and other insect pests are allergic to mint, and some of them, though not black aphids, are to nasturtiums.

Certain garden weeds also appear to be useful in the control of insect pests in the garden. Nettles are said to have a repellent effect on black aphids, and indeed an extract of nettle leaves can be used for spraying them. Most vegetables will grow more vigorously in the company of dead-nettles, but dandelions and buttercups have a depressing effect on most garden crops. With buttercups this is perhaps because of their strong growth and their greed for nitrogen, but it does seem that buttercups have an inhibiting effect on the production of nitrogen nodules by the roots of clover and other leguminous plants. Box is a poor companion plant of roses, though whether because of a chemical substance it produces or simply because its spreading roots compete with those of the roses is uncertain.

Lilies of the Valley are said to help most cut flowers to last longer in water, if placed in the same vase, but Gladioli have the opposite effect. Gladioli are bad plants to grow in a vegetable garden and are particularly antipathetic to leguminous plants. Oddly, a superstition has grown up that it is unlucky to put Gladioli in a sick-room.

It will be noted that many of the above statements are prefaced by the words 'It is said'! Research, though beginning, still has a long way to go, so amateurs have a chance of doing investigations on their own account. The following is a summary of the hints I have received so far on what to do and what to avoid.

Onions (also leeks and garlic) should be kept well clear of beans and other leguminous plants. It will, however, be helpful to beet and carrots, and lettuce will be beneficial to onions.

Beans and Peas will do well near most other crops, except those of the onion family, and are beneficial to cucumbers.

Cabbage is tolerant of most other plants, but strawberries do not like it. Celery and several herbs are said to help in keeping cabbage butterflies and aphids away from plants of the brassicas family. Kohl Rabi, which belongs to this family, has a depressing effect on tomatoes, although tomatoes and cabbage do well together.

Tomatoes and asparagus are mutually helpful.

Most salads grow well together, examples being lettuce and radishes, lettuce and spring onions, and lettuce and carrots. It is said that the flavour of radishes is improved by being grown near lettuce, and also by the proximity of nasturtiums, the leaves of which, of course, may be used as salad.

Leeks and celery do well together, and leeks are also good partners for carrots. Most gardeners sow spring cabbage or peas after lifting early potatoes, but potatoes grown in alternate rows with peas will benefit both crops. Potatoes and broad beans are also good companions, but not potatoes and tomatoes. Several plants, including raspberries, cucumbers and sunflowers, are said to make potatoes more susceptible to potato blight. Hemp, on the other hand, increases the resistance of potatoes to blight and also has a repellent effect on cabbage butterflies and other insect pests. It is, however, illegal to grow hemp – its other name is Cannabis!

Vegetable crops are usually grown in parallel rows, to make weeding as easy as possible, with one variety in each row. There is, however, much to be said for inter-cropping, that is growing several species of plants alternately in the same rows, provided one keeps apart those plants which have deleterious effects on each other. It will be gathered that a few plants of herbs at the end of or in vegetable ranks can be helpful, but beware fennel. A wise old gardener, Mr. Bill Sinnathanby, whom I met in Ceylon, insists that multiple cropping on these lines is the ideal even for agricultural crops. He likes to grow maize and other cereal crops in clearings in the forest surrounded by fruit trees with vanilla and pepper vines twining around them. But perhaps what is applicable in the forest culture of Sri Lanka is not quite the thing for us in open arable country.

Gardeners experimenting on these lines can come across some rather unusual effects. For instance, tomatoes seem to have a harmful effect on couch-grass and may be used to help clean a badly infested plot. Marigolds secrete, apparently, a chemical substance that destroys root eel-worms, which build up a bad infestation in land over-cropped with potatoes. Valerian, by a chemical reaction, tends to release phosphorus bound up in the soil.

It is worth repeating, however, that the study of this complex subject is still in its infancy, and there is quite a lot of interesting work that amateur gardeners can do to help it along.

Herb Tea

A West Moors reader told me she enjoys a cup of herb tea occasionally and makes it from various herbs, including thyme, fennel, lemon balm, mint and rosemary, but not sage. She has tried substitute coffee made from dandelion roots but liked it not at all.

'My father,' she wrote, 'used to love herbs. He had bunches drying all over the house. He needed guidance, though, for all he had was an old medical book that someone had given him. It had only a few poor pictures at the back – not good enough for identification. I remember he went out into the fields and picked a herb he thought was good for a cold cure. He made a strong brew and drank it.'

' "Lovely stuff," he pronounced. He didn't mind the bitter taste.'

'I wasn't happy about it, though, especially as it didn't look like the picture in his book. So I went to the library and borrowed a book about flowers. Then we were able to establish that what he had gathered was a herb recommended not for curing colds but for easing certain female complaints. My father nearly had a fit. He was more careful after that.'

She added another warning about the need for identifying wild plants correctly. Last year in a natural history exhibition she was showing some cinnabar moth caterpillars feeding on ragwort. The item created a lot of interest, but several people thought the ragwort flowers were coltsfoot. One woman was most disappointed at being assured that it was really ragwort.

'There's such a good crop of it about,' she said, 'and I was going to make coltsfoot wine with it. We were all sure it was coltsfoot.'

The possible effects of ragwort wine make one shudder to think about.

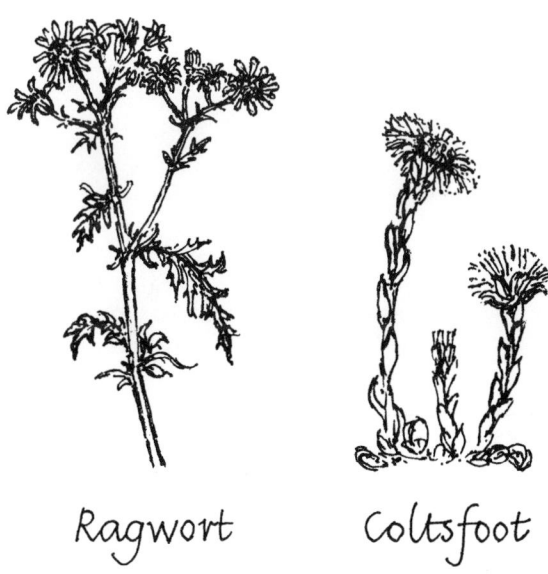

Ragwort   Coltsfoot

Tusser on Weeds

A Colyton reader passed on some verses she discovered on a scrap of paper hidden in an old drawer. She wondered what county dialect they represent.

'In May get a weed-hook, a crotch and a glove,
And weed out such weeds as the corn do not love.
In weeding of winter corn, now it is best;
But June is the better for weeding the rest.

'The May-weed doth burn and the thistle do fret;
The fitches pull downward both Rye and the Wheat.
The brake and the cockle be noisome too much,
Yet like unto boodle no weed there is such.

'Shirk never thy weeding, for dearth nor for cheap;
The Corn shall reward it, ere ever ye reap.
And specially where ye do trust for to seed,
Let that be well used, the better to speed.'

My correspondent has discovered a clue. Scribbled at the end of the verses is a name she has deciphered as Tusser. It looks like his work, too. Thomas Tusser was a farmer who wrote a book in verse, *Five Hundreth Points of Good Husbandrie*, in 1573. He was born in Essex, farmed in Suffolk and lived for many years in Suffolk, so the dialect is East Anglian.

My correspondent wondered about some of the words used and said that 'brake' and 'boodle' defeated her. 'Brake', I imagine, is bracken. 'Boodle' is the corn marigold. A 'crotch' is a forked stick, and 'fitches' would be vetches, though here presumably a wild variety. It is interesting to see this farmer of four hundred years ago recommending the hand-weeding of corn.

Onions and Garlic

A Holwell (Sherborne) reader sent me some tiny onion bulbs for identification. They were specimens of either the Egyptian or Tree Onion or the Potato Onion. The Tree Onion sends up a flower stalk which produces a cluster of tiny bulbs or bulbils at the top. The Potato Onion produces a similar cluster of small bulbs around the base of the stalk, just below the soil surface. Both types are good for flavouring, being decidedly 'strong'.

The same reader asked about the wild garlic, or ransoms – is it safe to use it? Yes, in the old days countrymen used to eat the leaves on bread-and-butter, especially in spring as a kind of tonic. They would also put a few leaves into a brandy bottle and allow them to steep for a time, again for use as a tonic. But it needs to be used sparingly, for, like the onions mentioned above, its flavour is very 'strong'. In the days when many herb medicines were concocted by distilling the essence of plants, it was calculated that a hundredweight of wild garlic leaves would be needed to procure three or four ounces of oil or essence.

Cattle also seem to appreciate the medicinal qualities of garlic, for they eat it readily in spring if allowed to – which, of course, they are not, for it taints their milk. Sheep, on the other hand, will not touch it.

Bedroom Water

In trying to explain to me why my runner beans gave such a disappointing crop in the previous year (a matter about which I had no doubt at all – they were short of water), an Amesbury reader offered some interesting items of old gardening lore. Having described the process of digging a trench, putting in a good layer of dung and sowing or transplanting the beans a few weeks later, he then suggested that a second trench be dug a few inches from the bean-sticks. Into this trench goes all the waste water from the household, every day, including what he called 'bedroom water', about which he wrote in glowing terms. The waste water naturally consisted largely of soapsuds, which he thought must have contained some ingredients of value to garden crops. I can confirm, from my own memories, that old-time gardens used to get plenty of them.

He went on to describe an old method of 'pickling' seed wheat. Urine was poured into a tub and allowed to stand for several weeks. The seed wheat was poured into a wicker basket and dipped into the liquor; then taken out to drain. When still damp, it was spread on a barn or outhouse floor and sprinkled with powdered chalk or carbonate of lime, which stuck to it. It was, he commented, an early form of pelleted seed!

He also asked whether I had ever tried stinging-nettle tea?

'A good spring tonic – rich in vitamins,' he recommended. 'You gather enough young nettles to fill a saucepan and boil as with cabbage greens. When cooked, eat the greens and drink the water, at half-a-pint a day. If you have a flint stone, boil this with them; it improves the flavour.'

Picking Fro-cups

A Lyme Regis reader tells me that since the last war she was shown a field full of fro-cups (fritillaries) in north-east Hampshire, near the Duke of Wellington's estate. As their existence became more widely known 'a gate was erected and a board added, with times of opening advertised and a small charge made for picking. As far as I know, the flowers are still there, probably now protected and with no picking allowed.'

She adds that nearby was the site of a Roman camp and that local people said that the fritillaries resembled Roman helmets.

An old friend told me that when first married she went to live near Aylesbury, where she was intrigued at being invited to take part in Fro-cup Sunday. The Fro-cup proved to be fritillaries, those now very rare flowers that bloom at that season. She and her husband walked to the village of Ford and paid threepence to enter a meadow, where they could pick as many as they liked. It was as well that they did it then, for today the fritillary is one of the rarest of British flowers. I believe its last localities are certain riverside meadows on the Wiltshire/Gloucestershire border, where it is preserved by the efforts of Wiltshire Trust for Nature Conservation. Pick a bunch of fritillaries there and you are likely to find yourself in Shepton Mallet jail!

How the attitude towards wildlife conservation has changed in my lifetime! In my first years at primary school I remember we were encouraged by our teachers to make expeditions to the cowslip meadows to gather big bunches of cowslips and bring to school, where we were shown how to make them into 'cowslip balls'. Now children would be taught that to do so is very wrong.

My friend told me that near the 'Fro-cup' field near Aylesbury was an inn in which were displayed pictures of a man dressed in green. Was this, she enquires, another reference to the dances and fertility rites of May? Undoubtedly it was. And there still is a Green Man somewhere in that part of England; I have had a meal there on more than one occasion.

Mighty Pumpkins

In the garden is there any plant more fragile or delicate than a trailing marrow or pumpkin? The long stems creep along the ground, weak as water, and seem unable even to support their own weight. But earlier in the summer I trained one of them (a pumpkin plant) to climb a wall, wedging the stem in a crevice so that it could not fall down. In due course it ran for a yard or two along the top of the wall, and I anchored it there at another spot. Then, between those two fixed points, it produced a pumpkin. Now the fruit must weigh at least twelve pounds, probably more, and is entirely supported by that one stem, which has grown thick and fibrous to stand the strain. The stem sags but it does not break; and I reckon that it would fortify itself to support any weight, no matter how heavy the fruit grew.

On Owning a Garden

Convalescing from an illness is like making a brief excursion back
to childhood. For a time you have been confined first to bed and
then to a couple of rooms in your house. Comes the day when,
cocooned in coats and scarves to an extent which you would
normally scorn, you venture outside and see above you the
immensity of the sky instead of a boxlike ceiling. The air is in
motion instead of stagnant, and it is filled with sound – for me the
gossipy chatter of the rooks and jackdaws in the tall trees over the
garden wall is predominant.

The garden seemed larger than I had realised. Apart from the
fact that to walk around it was about as much as I could manage
on my first excursion out-of-doors, I was surprised at the number
and variety of the plants it contained. What a wealth of
possessions!

I searched to see what flowers were in bloom on this crisp, cool,
sunny day in March that was providing a foretaste of Spring. I
found snowdrops, violets, one or two early daffodils, some
wallflowers, polyanthus, masses of pink bergenia, two clusters of
primula wanda, a thicket of hellebore well past its prime, an islet
of crocuses, and, picture-like in frames of grey stone walls, the pale
red japonica and the bright yellow forsythia. To complete the
tally, I looked for the little wild flowers that share the garden and
found daisies, celandines and groundsel. The yew tree in which a
starling sat singing was dripping pollen from its abundant
flowers.

I counted some of my botanical treasures and again was
surprised. There are far more than appear at first glance.
Wallflower plants, for instance, total 43; polyanthus, 42. And
then there are 120 sturdy canterbury bell plants, already forming
crowns in preparation for flowering. What a magnificent show
they will make in a few months' time. I double my pleasure at the
sight by visualising them now.

My stroll around the garden became a rendezvous with
memory. When I move house one of my first reconnaissances is
into the garden, to see what plants I have inherited, but also I
bring with me an accumulation of treasures from the past. So

now, as I peered into borders and corners with eyes that had
become accustomed to looking at little but books, television,
curtains and wallpaper, I thought of old friends who at various
times had given me the New Zealand fern which now resides
under the syringa bush, the autumn-flowering dwarf cyclamen,
the expanding clump of tall, lemon-coloured perennial scabious,
the rosemary bush, the meadow rue, the rock-plants I collected
from a garden in the Isle of Wight, and the hydrangea, a present
from one of our daughters last year. Plants and books are perhaps
the two best gifts. One never forgets the givers.

I was also struck by the free bonuses of our garden. A few years
ago I sowed a packet of borage seed, but I shall never need to buy
another for this garden. Borage plants, identifiable by their
rough, rounded leaves, are shooting up everywhere. Similarly I
never need to buy forget-me-not seed. I simply wait till the seed
has formed and then shake the plants over the garden when I pull
them up. There are always ample forget-me-nots in the following
spring. I noted a spinach-beet plant, above all things, shooting
vigorously from the top of a stone wall – now how on earth did that
get there, seeing that I have not allowed any spinach beet to seed?
I thought I had moved all my daffodils into the tubs which adorn
the front porch, but now I find still more about to bloom in the
plots where the bulbs were buried for the summer. As yet invisible
in the soil I know there are nasturtium, candytuft, linum and
many other seeds of annual plants which will appear in due
course.

Reflecting, I am amused to see how entirely possessive I have
been about these plants. I write as though they were all mine, but
the extent to which I own them is decidedly limited. There is a
difference between the annuals and the perennials, though I dare
say that even the annuals will be renewing themselves by self-
sown seed long after I have left this garden. But the perennials are
virtually everlasting. Pear-trees are proverbially planted for
posterity, and so are perennial flowers. I know an orchard where
every spring snowdrops flower which were planted by my
grandmother when she was first married, over a hundred years
ago. An apple tree planted by my great-grandfather still bears
fruit and looks remarkably healthy ... but its latest owner has been
pruning it and looking after it well

But does one really own trees or plants? When young I used to
think it would be fine to own a tree, but when eventually I did it

occurred to me that there wasn't much I could do with it. If it were an apple-tree I could pick the fruit, but a forest or ornamental tree can only be looked at. At the most, one can sit under its shade, which is a pleasure which can be enjoyed without ownership. The only way in which one can really exercise ownership of a tree is to cut it down – in which case one has destroyed one's possession. It is a curious situation.

If, on the other hand, I do not cut down my tree, then my ownership does not amount to much. At the most I have a temporary lease on it, for the tree is more permanent than I am. It will be there when I am gone, under the temporary control of some new 'owner'. Even the longevity of a forest tree, however, is insignificant compared to that of some of the lowly plants of the countryside. I know a south-facing woodland bank where every spring primroses bloom. They have done so ever since I can remember. And I wouldn't mind wagering that they were doing so long before Julius Caesar came to Britain.

Parsley Lore

I am intrigued by the strange folklore associated with parsley – the garden variety. It should apparently be sown at night, if not ideally, on Good Friday then when the moon is new, by the housewife rather than her husband, and the rows should run due north and south. It should never be transplanted or given away. If a neighbour wants some, let him help himself, preferably secretly, as though he were stealing. Parsley seed is difficult to start off, because it has to go down to Hell and back three times before it can germinate.

Who on earth thinks up these things?

While browsing over these remarkable facts I came across some others equally startling, some of which answer certain queries which have come my way over the past year or so. One was, I remember, concerned with the presence of monkey puzzle trees in the gardens of farms in, I think, a certain area of Somerset and west Dorset. Why were they planted? Well, I have discovered an old belief (though it cannot be all that old, for monkey puzzles were introduced from South America less than two hundred years ago) that they were planted to discourage the Devil from perching in them and watching the house! The Devil evidently loves a tree to perch in, so that he can note anything that happens to his advantage down below, but the monkey puzzle is altogether too uncomfortable for him.

Groundsel in the vegetable patch was attributed to witches. If that is true, there must still be a lot of witches about! I found a Fenland story of an old countryman who, 'when the sixth new moon was full', made a fire indoors, on the earth floor of his shack, of armfuls of dried groundsel he had been collecting all the spring. As it burned he kept it damped down with quarts of ale, till the place was filled with suffocating smoke and at last he was forced, coughing and choking, into the open. The alleged purpose of the operation was to smoke out any witches or evil spirits who happened to be lurking in the place, an aim which, after all, was probably achieved by suffocating a good proportion of the vermin infesting his clothes and bedding!

There is a Devon belief that it was unlucky to bring the first primroses indoors. This was probably associated with the other superstition that the number of flowers in the first bunch of primroses gathered would be the average number of chicken hatched by hens in the coming season. So the little girl who proudly trotted indoors to hand her mother the first solitary primrose of the year would understandably get her head clouted.

Chicory, too, features in folklore but in an unexpected form. It is said to be an aid to lock-picking. Working in complete silence a thief was advised to hold a leaf of chicory against the lock and to use a golden knife. It sounds unlikely, for if he could afford a golden knife it is doubtful whether he would be picking locks.

It is very unlucky to uproot daisies in bloom. An inexpensive form of fire insurance is to plant house-leeks on the roof of a house. Anyone wishing to sober up quickly before driving home from the pub should take a drink from a cup made of ivy-wood. Bring honeysuckle indoors and a wedding will soon follow. And I am intrigued by the frequent references to hemp in all manner of superstitions. Hemp seed features time and again, and when one remembers that the botanical name of hemp is *Cannabis* it seems decidedly significant. Hemp, of course, used to be grown as a field crop, for rope-making, and it is said that unmarried girls were forbidden to work in hemp-fields, lest it should make them infertile.

How to Grow Large Lettuce

To get extra large lettuce or cabbages, cut a slit in the stem just below the head when the head is about half-formed. It is not a bad idea to hold open the slit by means of a match-stick or sliver of wood. For some reason, this treatment seems to result in the head growing to a much larger size than usual.

Unpredictable Mushrooms

A Cerne Abbas reader was disappointed at finding no mush-rooms one autumn. In the previous year, he told me, he gathered over 20 pounds of them from a temporary grassfield (a three or four-years ley). Later the field was ploughed and produced a crop of grain. Although it remained undisturbed after harvest, no mushrooms grew.

The most frequent comment from his friends was 'Of course, you wouldn't expect it. Mushrooms grow only in undisturbed ground,' but he remains unconvinced. After all, a ley is only temporary grassland, and you grow cultivated mushrooms in well-worked compost.

Although I cannot answer the query of what prompts mushrooms suddenly to produce a crop where none has grown before, I can certainly dispose of the idea that they grow only in undisturbed soil.

In the last years of the war, when I was farming with my father in Wiltshire, we planted potatoes in a fourteen-acre field. It was on land traditionally arable but which from time to time was laid down to grass, and I suppose that back in the 1920s it had been derelict for a time. At the tail-end of harvest, when we were beginning to think about lifting the potatoes, we went one day to inspect the field and found it bearing a prodigious crop of mushrooms!

There were mushrooms everywhere. They were growing on the ridges and between the ridges, and many of them, of the same colour as the soil, were difficult to detect. The more you searched, the more you found. We left a team to finish the corn harvest and set the rest of the staff gathering this bonus crop. Over the next week or two they gathered, on estimate, nearly two tons.

Next year there were just a few, and after that, nothing. We could not remember there ever having been mushrooms in that field before, though perhaps there may have been just a few. Potatoes were then a new field crop on English farms, grown to meet wartime needs, and we were allowed allocations of special manures, rich in potash, to help in growing them. We were inclined to give credit for our mushrooms to these potash manures, but, although we later used the same manures to grow crops of potatoes on similar fields, they never again produced a crop of mushrooms.

So the matter remains a mystery. Where mushroom mycelium is dormant in the soil, it can remain so for a long time, until certain conditions trigger off a harvest, but what those conditions are we still don't know.

Later a Yeovil reader recalled an incident in the Pendomer district a few years earlier.

'These farmers had a crop of kale, through which they left a wide path as a short cut for the dairy herd at milking time. After the crop was cleared, mushrooms galore came up where the path had been – basketfuls. There were none elsewhere in the field and there had never been any in that strip of it before.'

Another letter came from Whitsbury, near Fordingbridge, which, my correspondent reminded me, is a village with more horses than people.

'One would expect a reasonable crop of mushrooms each autumn,' he wrote, 'but none appeared this autumn or last, though rings of *horse mushrooms* cropped regularly for many weeks. However, in the late September and early October of 1976, following the long hot summer, mushrooms grew here in great abundance. Virtually every field in the parish bore a crop. The same thing happened in the autumn of 1959 and, I believe, 1946, both of which years enjoyed hot summers.

'Mushroom growth would therefore seem to require certain weather conditions, namely, a prolonged period of very warm weather, which dries out and heats the soil, followed by a few days of heavy rain and falling temperatures.'

I would agree with that. In some instances, however, other factors are involved. In the example quoted above, the consolidation of the soil by the cows' hooves would seem to have played a part.

TIMES PAST

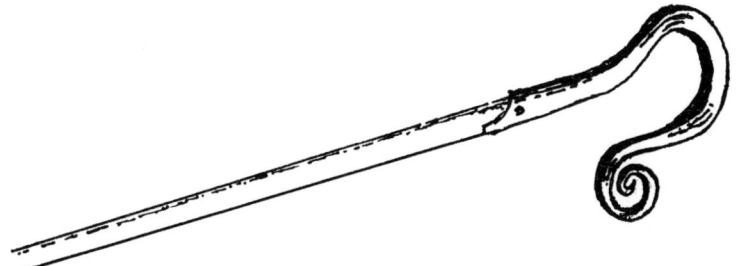

Old Time Sheep Fairs

With harvest finished, we are now in the middle of the season of autumn fairs. They were originally of three sorts, namely, *charter fairs*, which were established by a charter granted by some king or another, *statute fairs*, established by statute for the exchange of commodities, including labour, and traditional *sheep fairs*, often held at convenient centres remote from human population, where they needed neither charter nor statute. Both statute and sheep fairs were associated with Michaelmas, the statute fairs because that was when farms changed hands and workers changed jobs, the sheep fairs because they were necessary for the disposal of surplus stock at that season. Michaelmas has, however, two dates, the present one of September 29th and the old one, belonging to the period before the calendar was changed (in 1752), October 10th. Many fairs stick to the old date, and others have been dispersed to other dates around the same point of the calendar.

Weyhill Fair, near Andover, now discontinued, was one of the great autumn sheep fairs of Wessex and was held on Old Michaelmas. Back in the 18th century it was said that during this fair more than £300,000 changed hands for sheep alone, and that was when sheep were fetching 12 shillings each. Reputed to be even larger in its heyday, St. Giles Fair at Winchester extended over sixteen days around September 12th. It was a charter fair (the charter granted by King William Rufus), and one of the stipulations was that while it was being held no business could be transacted at any other place within seven leagues' radius. It was like a temporary city, say old records, whole streets of booths being erected, each for the sale of a particular commodity.

St. Giles's, like many old fairs, was held not in the city but on the top of a neighbouring hill, which suggests that, although it was established by royal charter, it may have been in existence long before that. These hill-top fairs, of which Westbury, Yarnbury Castle and Cold Berwick Hill (near Berwick St. Leonard) were examples, were, above all else, convenient centres for the great flocks of sheep that roamed the chalk downs. They may have been held on the same sites since prehistoric times, and Yarnbury Castle, on the hills above Wylye, was actually penned (on October 4th) within the ramparts of an Iron Age earthwork.

At Wilton Great Fair (on September 12th) the shepherds of Salisbury Plain used to assemble on the evening prior to the Fair and contend for the title 'King of the Shepherds'. It was not a contest of skill in shepherding but a straightforward fight, in which the weapons were cudgels, fists and boots, and no holds were barred. The battles over, the shepherds slept on the barn floor in a circle, feet outwards and heads resting on their most valuable possession, their dogs.

A similar fight, though not for such a resounding title, used to be staged regularly at Hurstbourne Priors, near Andover, where shepherds of Hampshire, Wiltshire and Somerset fought each other with cudgels ('shepherds' sticks'). Here certain basic rules were laid down; the contestants might strike each other anywhere except on the face, and the fight ended when the first blood was drawn.

Another West Country Fair, Sherborne Fair, has stuck to Old Michaelmas. It was, or is, known as Pack Monday Fair, possibly a reference to the packs of pedlars in mediaeval times, though a local tradition says it commemorates an occasion when workmen building the Abbey packed up work in order to go to the Fair. Formerly it was heralded by the ringing of a great bell in the early hours and by boys patrolling the streets and blowing cows' horns.

Some of the Devonshire fairs were known as Glove Fairs, because their opening was marked by the hoisting of a glove on a decorated pole. Others were Mop Fairs or Giglet Fairs. These were the statute fairs, where labourers sought work contracts for the coming year. Traditionally they stood around, each wearing the emblems of their craft or trade – a tuft of wool for a shepherd, whipcord for a carter, straw or cow's hair for a cowman, a mop for a maid. A writer of 1883 commented, 'Young girls dressed in their finest clothes were exhibited like cattle to be hired by the would-be employers, who came to the fair to seek their services.'

One of the West Country's obsolete fairs, which will, however, never be forgotten as long as Thomas Hardy's novels live, was Woodbury Hill Fair. This was another hill-top fair, held near Bere Regis for about five days from, I think, September 18th. It was so important that documents were dated from 'Woodbury Fair' in villages for ten or fifteen miles around. Once, in 1648, a public thanksgiving in Dorchester was postponed because 'it falls out to be on Woodbury Fair Eve, at which time most of the Towne will be from home.'

One of the interesting features of the Fair was the vast area from which people came to the Fair. Having given details of a case of theft, in which the persons involved came from London, Salisbury and Coventry, the author states that other traders included 'a mercer from Honiton in Devon, two chapmen from Coventry, a weaver from Devon who had come to the fair to sell cloth and to buy cheese, a shoemaker and a pack-saddle maker from Wells, bonelace sellers from Berkshire and Oxfordshire, as well as people from all over Dorset and the neighbouring counties.'

Joanna Southcott's Box

A Blandford reader posed the query, Has anyone yet opened Joanna Southcott's Box? And is it still in existence?

Yes, I believe it is still in existence, at Bedford. And I have never heard that it has been opened. In fact, unless someone has been remiss in carrying out the terms of her will it has almost certainly not, for she insisted that it should remain locked until twenty-four bishops had been brought together to witness the opening, and I cannot imagine that twenty-four bishops have ever lent themselves to such a ceremony. Perhaps it is a pity, for, according to tradition, when the Box is opened it will be found to contain a panacea for all the ills of the world, and wars, quarrels, conflict and poverty will cease.

It is perhaps not generally known that Joanna Southcott, a lady of the calibre of Old Moore, was a West Country lady. She was, in fact, the daughter of a peasant farmer of Gittisham, in east Devon and spent most of her life, until the age of forty, in service in Exeter. She then fell under the influence of a travelling revivalist preacher, who used to play so much on the emotions of his congregation that sometimes he would have the whole company 'flat and rigid on the floor, when he would walk in and out among them and revive them by assuring them they had received pardon for all their sins, were elect vessels and that their election had been sealed in Heaven'.

After a thorough indoctrination on these lines, Joanna herself began to see visions and to be visited by spirits, who revealed to her that she was the Woman referred to in the twelfth chapter of the Book of Revelation and would in due course become the mother of the second Messiah, whose name would be Shiloh. She began issuing prophecies galore, the most important of which, however, she placed in sealed packets and handed to a Methodist minister for safe keeping. When, however, she starred to circulate the claim that, on the strength of accepting the packets, he was one of her disciples, he became alarmed and, unwisely, burnt the packets. It was a providential act for Joanna, for thenceforth she would claim that this and that event had certainly been foretold but that the proof was lacking because the minister had burnt it!

In addition, she and her adherents, who were now increasing daily, harassed and abused the poor man beyond measure.

As time went on, she issued more and more prophecies, which she sold. She also cashed in on copies of letters of denunciation which she sent to the minister and other transgressors; and she even sold sealed passports to Heaven, at twelve shillings and one guinea each. By the time of her death, in 1814, her followers numbered certainly more than one hundred thousand, in all parts of England.

Earlier in that year she announced that she was pregnant, and she had already said that when her time came she would lie as though dead for four days, after which she would be revived and be delivered of the child, the second Messiah. So when, just after Christmas, she really did die her followers confidently expected her to rise again in four days' time. In fact, she never was pregnant; the cause of death was given as dropsy. Faith in her did not waver, however, for long afterwards, and fifty years later there were still people, especially around her native east Devon, who were awaiting her resurrection.

Apart from her own semi-literate ramblings, which were voluminous, books beyond measure were written about her. And her bequest to posterity is still apparently intact. Her famous Box has, however, been X-rayed and is known to contain a pistol, as well as other unidentified objects. I used to hear her talked about when I was a boy.

Heirlooms & Bygones

A visit to the Bell Inn at Luckington, in the north-west corner of Wiltshire, prompted me to rummage in my own collection of agricultural bygones and to make plans for displaying them properly. For Mr. Owen, mine host at the Bell (incidentally, one of the nearest hostelries to Badminton), has collected an impressive assortment of farming and domestic tools, implements, utensils and suchlike within the space of less than two years. His collection started, quite unpremeditatively, with some items of horses' harness and has just snowballed, until now almost every available space on the walls and ceilings is jam-packed with impedimenta.

Whenever I see a collection such as this I am filled with a sense of nostalgia, for it seems to me that I have used about half the exhibits, never dreaming that within my lifetime they would become museum pieces. There are scythes and assorted bill-hooks and reap-hooks, prongs and forks of various designs, dairy equipment, shepherds' tools and a wide selection of horse-gear. There are pots and pans, shop scales like those on which my Aunt Polly used to weigh out loaf sugar and pennyworths of sweets, carriage lamps such as we had on our pony-trap before we acquired our first car in 1921, stone jars galore, some massive bellows from a smithy, and flat-irons for heating in front of an open fire. Outside, a bonding-plate, once used for forcing iron bonds on to wooden waggon wheels, is cemented into a stone wall. Anyone in the vicinity of Luckington could spend an interesting hour browsing through Mr. Owen's collection, as well as getting a first-rate meal in the bargain.

Mind you, collecting rural antiques seems to be a popular occupation of village pubs, and readers will doubtless know where they can see some similar hoard, though perhaps not of such dimensions. Indeed, when writing my book, *Gentle Giants*, I originally suggested that, in view of the problem and expense in obtaining harness for heavy horses nowadays, probably the best move would be to raid a country pub! Then I re-worded it, lest anyone should take the recommendation seriously.

Anyhow, returning home I checked up to remind myself of the flotsam that had been washed up on my stretch of beach. I am quite addicted to my collection of sheep-bells and horse-bells. Some of the former I was still using in the early 1960s, but most of the latter were made over 200 years ago, by Robert Wells, of Aldbourne. I have my father's sheep-crook and sundry other tools. A mud-walling prong, with which Wiltshire countrymen used to make chalk cob walls – a lost art. There is a straw bee-skep; a Roman horse-shoe; a shepherd's smock; a plough-bottle; a particularly good example of a corn dolly; my mother's butter-pats and a host of other items. But sometimes when I think of the things that at various times we threw away, gave away, smashed or burned I feel like kicking myself. I remember King George V's Jubilee. I wonder what happened to all the souvenirs we were given then?

One family heirloom which spends the years folded between tissue-paper in a moth-proof drawer is a christening dress. I gather that one of my great-grandmothers was in service in London in, I imagine, the 1830s, and when she came back to Wiltshire to settle down and marry, two of the ladies in her former employer's home made this exquisite piece of needlework for the christening of the first baby. It is beautifully embroidered, looks like lace and must have taken them weeks if not months to sew. Since then almost every member of our family has been christened in it, and we trust to hand it on to future generations.

I suspect that very many families treasure similar heirlooms, something of sentimental value that has belonged to ancestors. I remember once being entertained in a cottage in North Devon and, admiring a couple of paintings on the parlour wall, was startled to see that they were signed by Sir Alfred Munnings.

'Oh yes, he stayed here for a time when he was painting,' said my hostess, 'and he gave us those to remember him by.'

They must have been worth a fortune ... but what am I saying? What value can one put on such things? Which is the more important – cash value or sentimental value? In my years of travelling in the tropical world I came face to face with limitless suffering. People starved not because there was a shortage of food but because they had no money with which to buy it; they fell ill, became blind or died, not because there were no remedies but because they could not afford to pay for them. What is of more value than a human life? Practically everything, in modern cash terms.

And why translate everything into cash values? This American attitude, of assessing everything according to its dollar equivalent, has got out of hand. I confess to being a little shocked when I read of parents protesting because they have been given only, say, £500 for the accidental death of a small child. Presumably they regard such a small sum as an insulting estimate of the child's value. But no sum on earth would compensate for the loss of a much-loved child. Why try to put a cash value on it?

In Africa I encountered many tribes just getting to grips with the modern world and trying to understand a cash economy. They had never previously had to deal with money. They would be wiser to have nothing to do with it.

Like the West African farmer I found sitting with his feet up under the shade of a mango-tree one hot afternoon. The following conversation ensued.

Myself: 'I hear your yams and maize did well last year.'

African: 'They were good. We had enough.'

Myself: 'That was on four acres. Seeing you've done so well, why don't you expand? Why not cultivate eight acres this year?'

African: 'Then what would I be doing on a hot afternoon like this? Out in the sun, cultivating my crops. And I would make myself ill, and who would look after me?'

Myself: 'But everything you produced on the extra four acres would be surplus. You could afford to pay someone to help you. And you would have money to spare for buying all sorts of things.'

African: 'What things?'

Myself: 'We-ell, a bicycle ... a transistor radio ... a new suit ... surely there's something you want?'

African: 'Yes, I want to be able to sit under this mango-tree on hot afternoons, doing nothing! Now buzz off ...'

Or words to that effect. It wasn't until quite a time afterwards that I realized what a wise man I had met that day.

The Good Old Days?

Washington Irving's description of Christmas in times past (see pages 155-157) gives only half the picture. Washington Irving was a guest at a country house Christmas, a festival with all the trappings and good cheer beloved by romantic novelists, and he cheerfully assumed that the same sort of festivity, on a minor scale, was in progress down in the cottages of the village. It was not necessarily so.

Just before Christmas, 1837, a worthy citizen of Andover, Hugh Mundy, distressed by the near-starvation which prevailed in Andover Workhouse, wrote to ask the Poor Law Commissioners to allow the inmates a Christmas dinner. One gathers that he and some of his friends were willing to supply at least some of the ingredients. The reply he received was as follows:-

'The Poor Law Commissioners for England and Wales regret that they do not feel justified in assenting to the proposition ... that the paupers of the Union Workhouse should be regaled on the ensuing Christmas Day with a good Dinner and Beer, to be provided at the expense of the Guardians and others willing to contribute by voluntary subscriptions.

'The Commissioners consider that this proposition is directly at variance with the principles upon which the efficacy of the Workhouse System depends, namely, that the condition of the pauper inmate of the Workhouse should not be desired or envied by the independent person; and the Commissioners therefore cannot consent that the inmates of the Workhouse should be supplied with indulgencies which too many of those who support themselves without parochial aid are obliged altogether to forgo.'

The principles on which the efficacy of the Workhouse System depends had been faithfully enunciated a few years earlier. 'The Workhouse should be a place of hardship, of coarse fare, of degradation and humility; it should be administered with strictness – with severity; it should be as repulsive as is consistent with humanity. . .'

The idea, of course, was to make it so objectionable that no-one who could possibly avoid it would enter the doors. Thus the poor rates would be kept down.

The Poor Law Commissioners' letter implies that they were well aware that things were not much better outside. Far from enjoying the sort of Christmas dinner that Washington Irving describes, most of the cottagers were not getting 'a good Dinner and Beer'.

Incidentally, the official diet for the inmates of Andover Workhouse at that time was, for males over nine years of age:- 6 ounces of bread and $1\frac{1}{2}$ pints of gruel for breakfast; 7 ounces of bread and 2 ounces of cheese for dinner; 6 ounces of bread and $1\frac{1}{2}$ ounces of cheese for supper.

Women had rather less. Once a week the paupers had meat for dinner – 8 ounces of it, together with half-a-pound of vegetables; and once a week 5 ounces of bacon and half-a-pound of vegetables. On those days, of course, they had no bread and cheese for dinner. For misdemeanours the ration was halved.

Nine years later, in 1846, we find the dauntless Hugh Mundy proposing that, as Christmas Day fell on a bread-and-cheese day and that as the authorities would not allow roast beef and plum pudding to be supplied by public subscription, it should be reckoned as a meat day. There was no seconder for his proposition.

The workhouse system endured for the rest of the century and well into the present century. For generations of agricultural labourers it was an ever-present bogey. My father remembered that when minor disasters occurred in his home his mother, a widow with three small children to support, would burst into tears and exclaim, 'Oh dear, now we shall all have to go to the workhouse!' By the time the villagers I knew as a boy had grown old the system had changed. I remember that some of them, ill and incontinent, were transferred at last to an old people's home. But the buildings were the old workhouse buildings, and the old folk went unwillingly. As far as they were concerned, they were going to the workhouse. Even now the shadows linger. I feel sure they deter many old people from applying for the social security benefits to which they are entitled.

So, there were Christmasses and Christmasses in the old days, graded according to social status.

The other day a septuagenarian provided me with a breakdown of local employment when he was a boy at the village of Sutton Montis, tucked under the ramparts of Cadbury Castle. Out of a population of about 140, 57 found regular employment within the village. There were four farms, employing 17 adults and 6 youths. These farms together with a dairy also employed 3 cheesemakers, and two more adults and one youth also worked in the dairy. Three 'big houses' found work for five gardeners, three grooms, one chauffeur, ten indoor staff and two other men. The rectory employed a gardener and two indoor staff; and there were two schoolteachers. In addition to these regular employees there existed a population of casual independent workers who engaged in such tasks as apple-picking (the village had 72 acres of orchards), hoeing, thatching and haymaking.

The picture is of a self-contained rural community from which the old pressures, such as those which created the workhouses, had more or less vanished. It was too good to last, and the first world war rang its death-knell. At present fewer than ten persons find employment in the village. As with so many West Country parishes, without commuters and retired people the place would be dead.

Incidentally, visiting a big estate not long ago I was shown the head gardener's house, built in Victorian times, which had been designed for a household with at least two servants. Two servants for a gardener!

Still harking back to a previous age, on Boxing Day I was intrigued by what I found on a visit to Minstead church, in the New Forest. Here are three Georgian 'parlour pews', constructed for important local families in the days when each was expected to have its family pew. These were, however, a stage in advance of the normal, for they were very like private boxes in a theatre, and each had its own outside entrance. Each was also equipped with its own fireplace and furnishings, the latter including in one instance a sofa. At one time the entire south wall of the church was taken down to enlarge the squire's pew.

Above one of the parlour pews, high under the roof, is a gallery, the purpose of which had me wondering. It was, I learned, built in 1818 to provide free seats for a local charity school and for the poor of the parish. Later it became known as 'The Gipsies' Gallery', doubtless because it was used by New Forest gipsies.

Like other New Forest churches, this is a fascinating building, rich in ancient woodwork and quaint features. There are three bells, the oldest dating back to the fifteenth century, and an oak gallery for musicians, a Norman or Saxon font with curious carvings, and a three-decker pulpit. The Forest churches have a homely atmosphere, perhaps because there is so much timber in their construction. Is it because board floors, steps and furnishings are more like home than their stone counterparts in the stately Somerset churches?

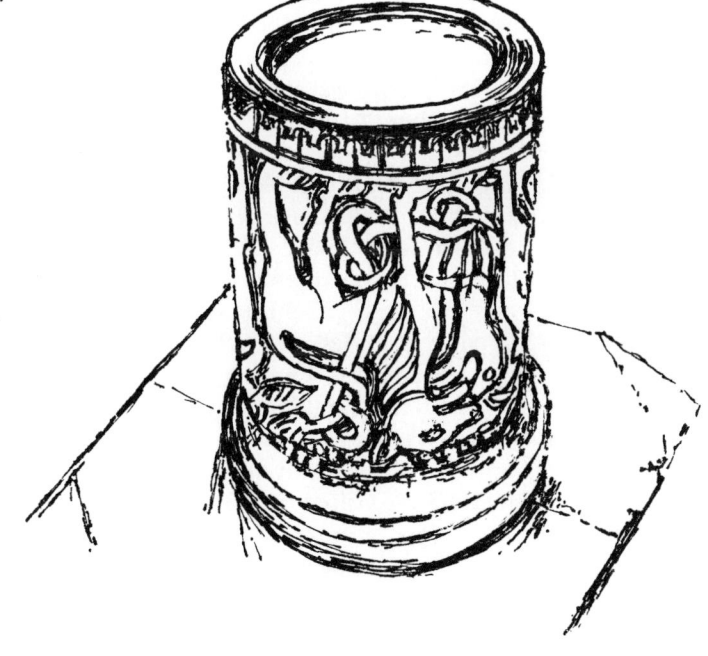

Century Spanners

In November 1975, a Yeovil reader passed on to me some memories of his uncle who died within the past two or three years, aged about 87. This old man was born at Devizes, where his father had a leather business. The father intended that the boy should follow in the family trade, but the boy had other ideas. He ran away and joined the Navy, where he served for many years, as a *sail-maker*. That word is significant, for it implies that he was in the Navy when at least some sailing ships were still in service.

On one voyage he went to Australia, where he met an old sheep farmer who recognised, by his accent, that he was a West Country man. They fell into conversation and discovered that both were natives of Devizes.

'How did you come out here?' he asked the old farmer.

'In a convict ship,' was the reply.

The old chap had, when young, been transported for some minor offence, in the days when transportation was still a common punishment, and had stayed on to become a prosperous sheep farmer.

Before he left his father's leather business at Devizes, the sail-maker could remember loads of bison skins coming into the tannery. This must have been at the time when settlers were pouring westwards over the great plains of the United States and Canada and slaughtering the herds of bison by thousands. Until about 1860 there were an estimated 60 million bisons in the West, but by about 1900 only 300 were left in the States and about 500 in Canada. The chief decades of slaughter were the 1870s and 1880s. Evidently shiploads of hides were then sent to Bristol and distributed about the country. Our informant recalled the great thickness of the skin on the shoulders or hump – 'several inches; it had to be pared down before you could use it.'

I also received a letter from a lady at Corfe Mullen who is nearly 91 years old. In 1903 she visited the battlefield of Waterloo and was shown around Hougoumont Farm (which was at the centre of the battle) by the niece of the man who was farming it when the battle took place in 1815! She was born a few years after the battle but had absorbed all the details about it from her relations, and she was particularly full of information about the defence of the farm by the Highlanders, whose exploits she recounted with pride.

Another of her memories is of visiting, in 1911, 'an old General, a relative of my husband, who, as a twenty-year-old officer, was in the Residency at Lucknow during its long siege in the Indian Mutiny of 1857. He showed me many photos he took during the siege.'

More Army reminiscences come from a Misterton reader who has himself had a distinguished career in the Army and who used, in his boyhood days, to listen to stories told by his grandmother of her father's exploits.

'From 1906 to 1911 I spent my school holidays with my grandmother in Dulverton. She ardently wished me to join the - Army and told me many stories related to her when a child by her father. He was commissioned from the Royal Military Academy into the Royal Regiment of Artillery in November, 1799. I followed him in 1916 and saw his name on the boards in the Library. He served in Egypt (1801/03), South America (1806/07), Portugal, Spain and France (1809/14) and U.S.A. (1814/15). He was "awarded his jacket", and I have a miniature portrait of him wearing it. He commanded the Rocket Company for the invasion of southern France and was awarded a gold medal for it.'

My correspondent will have some memories of his own to pass on to future generations, for in February, 1942, he escaped with a small party from Singapore in a leaky boat, which was kept afloat for over forty miles by continuous bailing. Later he served for over a year under General Eisenhower and made the first British crossing of the Rhine on the night of March 23/24, 1945.

Yet another set of reminiscences, from a Manston (Sturminster Newton) resident, are mostly concerned with London. They are the memories of my informant's grandfather, who died some time ago aged ninety-one.

'His father had kept a flock of 1,000 ewes in Hertfordshire, but when he lost them with, I believe, foot-and-mouth disease, his son set off for London to make his fortune.

He opened a business as a butcher in Kensington, on the site of the present Earls Court Station. This must have been about 1850. I well remember him telling me, when I was a young man, of losing seven fat beasts which were wandering on his grazing land just off Kensington High Street and not finding them for several days. He was the first man to drive along Cromwell Road when it was opened.

I myself can well remember seeing Highland cattle grazing in the park of Holland House, just off Kensington High Street, some fifty years ago.'

A reader told me that her grandmother, who was born in 1854, was taught needlework in 1860 by the youngest sister of Lord Nelson!

These reminiscences led to my discussing with some friends how human memory can span the centuries. The instance that raised the topic was a passage I read in S. Baring-Gould's *A Book of the West*, written in 1899. In it he quotes an interview with an old gentleman, 'very advanced in age', in 1880, who had heard his father talking of old men he knew who had been eye-witnesses of the landing of the Prince of Orange (William III) at Torbay in 1688.

Supposing the old man was 80 years old in 1880, his memories of his father's reminiscences would date from about 1810. Old men who, as boys, saw William III and his Dutch troops land in 1688 could well have lived till 1760 or 1770. So, if the old man's father was born in 1750 or 1760, the thing is demonstrably possible.

Quite a lot of detail, which helped to make the event come alive after so many years, was passed on in this way. One of the old men remembered that the horses walked already harnessed off the ships. Another that some of the horses were dropped overboard and swam to shore, 'guided by only a single rope running from the ship to the shore'.

'My father,' says the 1880 veteran, 'remembered one Gaffer Will Webber, of Staverton, who lived to a great age, say that he went from Staverton as a boy with his father, who took a cartload of apples from Staverton to the highroad from Brixham to Exeter, that the soldiers might help themselves to them and to wish them "Godspeed".'

I think that the most remarkable instance I have come across personally of bridging the centuries concerns an old lady I met in south Devon in, I believe, 1951. She showed me a medal that her father had won at the Battle of Waterloo, in 1815! The explanation is that her father was a drummer-boy, of about fifteen, when he participated in the battle. He married for a second time late in life and had a second family, of whom this lady was the youngest. Thus the span of 150 years is easily bridged.

My father, who was born in 1874, said that old men alive when he was a boy had told him they could remember when the steep chalk hillside above my native Wiltshire village was ploughed by breast-plough, often pulled by women, with a man behind guiding it. This must have been during the Napoleonic Wars.

When in my teens I found a reference in an old survey of an isolated forester's house (with barns and 'a little house for storing nuts') on an estate near my home I went to see if I could identify the place and thought I could discern traces of wall foundations, The latest reference dated from the time of Queen Elizabeth I, but later an uncle of mine told me that when he was a boy he worked with an old man who could just remember when the ruins of the house were still visible.

A few miles away is a hill-top track which in former days – a very long time ago – linked the local Roman road with the mediaeval Clarendon Palace. The Palace fell into ruin probably during the period of the Wars of the Roses, five hundred years ago. Before that it was a favourite hunting lodge of the kings of England, and many a party of horsemen must have cantered along that track from what was then the highway. So perhaps it is not surprising that, when I was a boy, I used to hear ghost stories of men on horses passing that way on dark nights. It was a case of inherited memories passing into legend as the time they were concerned with became more and more remote.

A Redlynch (Salisbury) reader wrote, however, to correct one of the reminiscences quoted above.

'I was interested to read of your correspondent's link with Lord Nelson's youngest sister, but I am afraid that the latter could not have taught anyone needlework in 1860. Lord Nelson's youngest sister, Catherine (Mrs. George Matcham), was my great-great-grandmother. She died in Kensington in 1842 and is buried at Slaugham Church, Sussex.

She *was* a notable needlewoman, and specimens of her work are still preserved in the family. She passed on her talent to her daughters, two of whom outlived her. One, Mrs. Horatio Mason, lived until 1869, and I believe another, Mrs. Montgomery Moore, was alive then, too. So perhaps it was one of these whom your correspondent's grandmother knew.'

That, I think, is the likely explanation.

A quite remarkable instance of a Century Spanner was given

me by a Somerton friend:-

'In the mid 1930s the octogenarian squire Robert Neville Grenville, of Butleigh Court, Glastonbury, remembered, as a small boy, meeting a very old woman in Compton Dundon around 1855. She told him that, when a child, a great grandparent had spoken to her about the battle of Sedgmoor (1685) and could recall hearing shots being fired there.'

Supposing that the old woman was ninety in 1855, she could have been talking with her great grandparents just before 1765, and if the great grandparent was then aged about ninety, the thing is possible.

Then I had a letter from an East Coker reader who has remembered the story, said to be true, of how an old lady at dinner with the Duke of Wellington (the 'Iron Duke' of the battle of Waterloo fame) heard the Duke make a disparaging remark about Oliver Cromwell, and retorted,

'Not at all, my late husband's first wife's first husband knew him intimately and had a high opinion of him.'

This dinner probably took place after the battle of Waterloo, say 1820, so we have to span the years between that date and the 1650s, Oliver Cromwell dying in 1658. With some young-to-old marriages it is possible. I have worked out the sequence as follows:-

Supposing the old lady was in her eighties in 1820. She would thus have been born in the 1740s and probably married in the 1760s. She must have married an elderly man, born perhaps in the 1690s, – but such an event is not unheard of. The husband had been married before. We can assume that this happened between 1710 and 1720, when he was in his twenties. He married a lady who had been married before and was older than he – therefore probably an heiress. We will say that she was in her forties and was therefore born in the 1670s. Her first marriage would thus probably take place in the 1690s and, as she became a widow not too many years afterwards, we can assume that this was to an older man. And a man who knew Oliver Cromwell in the 1650s need be no more than about sixty in the 1690s.

And so the centuries are spanned!

Well, how far back can you go with stories told to you when you were very young? It would be interesting to know if we have any other century-spanners among our readers.

We come again to faulty memories, and a Wells reader has

pointed out an error in the memories of our correspondent who visited the battlefield of Waterloo in 1903. 'The Highland regiments who fought at Waterloo did *not* defend Hougoumont Farm, as stated, but held the ridge to the east of La Haye Sainte. Hougoumont was defended by the flank companies of the 2nd and 3rd battalions of the First Guards (now the Grenadier Guards), the flank company of the 2nd battalion of the Coldstream Guards and the flank company of the second battalion of the Third Guards (now the Scots Greys).'

Details tend to fade with the years, though the basic facts remain vivid.

An Early Migrant to Australia

A Plymstock (Devon) reader sent a photograph of a tombstone she recently spotted when visiting her son in Australia. It was in the tiny settlement of Bicheno in a remote and lonely part of east-south-east Tasmania. The inscription reads:-

'In affectionate remembrance of JOHN ALLEN, who departed this life 19th December, 1879, aged 75 years. Native of Somerset, England. Arrived in Tasmania 1826. Fought a tribe of Aborigines single-handed on the 14th December 1828. Shipwrecked among the Ice off Cape Horn whilst going to England on 21st June 1832.'

A pious verse follows, and the tombstone also records the death of John Allen's wife, Anne, who died on October 18th, 1926, aged 92 years.

Apart from the interest to any readers who may be able to claim relationship with this intrepid pioneer, I find it interesting to think of young John Allen venturing out from Somerset as one of the first settlers in a virtually unknown land. The very first English colony was established there only in 1804, twenty-two years before John arrived, and that was a penal colony. It is to be hoped that he did not have to make the voyage unwillingly, in a convict ship. He must have been one of the last persons ever to have seen a Tasmanian aborigine, for by the middle of the nineteenth century the race had been exterminated by white settlers. Incidentally, if you work it out you will see that his wife was thirty years younger than he was.

Maintaining the Cerne Abbas Giant

Traditionally, the 'scouring' as it was called, of the Cerne Abbas
Giant was carried out by the local inhabitants. It was supposed to
take place every seven years, which would be about right for good
maintenance, but the period was somewhat elastic. I have no
details of what went on at Cerne, but presumably it would have
been much the same as at scourings of other white horses, about
which considerable information exists. There is even a book, *The
Scouring of the White Horse*, written in 1857 (and therefore now
probably unobtainable) by Thomas Hughes, at the request of the
committee then responsible for the work of restoring the White
Horse at Uffington. Though written as a novel, the book gives a
detailed account of the event.

The scouring was associated with what was euphemistically
referred to as a 'pastime'. The items included 'a jingling match,
wrestling, foot races, hurdle races, a race of cart-horses in thill
harness, a donkey race (for a flitch of bacon), climbing a greasy
pole (for a leg of mutton), catching a loose pig, racing down the
hill for a cheese.' That was in 1857. An earlier schedule, for a
scouring in 1776, was more adventurous. The horse races and foot
races were there as in 1857, also the cart-horse race (with the
stipulation that the horses were to be ridden, without saddles, by
carters in smock frocks) and the donkey race. But then we find a
waistcoat, valued at 10 shillings and 6 pence, offered as a prize for
the man who could in the shortest time retrieve a bullet from a
barrel of flour, using his mouth only. And a 'good hat to be run for
by men in sacks, every man to bring his own sack.' And 'cudgel-
playing, for a gold-laced hat'. Other novelties were an event
called 'grinning through a horse-collar' and a smoking race, with
a prize of half-a-guinea or a gallon of gin for the woman who could
smoke most tobacco in an hour! Accessories were stalls 'all decked
out with nuts and apples and gingerbread, and all sorts of sucks
and food, and children's toys, and cheap ribbons, knives, braces,
straps and all manner of gaudy-looking articles ... ' There were
acrobats and other performers, and 'every show had its own

music, if it were only a drum and pan-pipes, and all the musicians were playing, as loud as they could play, different tunes. Then, on the east side, were the great booths of the publicans, all decked out now with flowers and cheap flags, with their skittle-grounds behind; and lots of gipsies and other tramps, with their "three sticks a penny" and other games.'

Obviously a very lively occasion. The affair lasted for two days, which gave people time both to enjoy themselves and to do some work on the Horse. An illustration in Hughes' book shows a score or two of men busily ramming chalk into the Horse's outline.

The general tendency of a hillside figure is to slip downhill, as the rain washes away the chalk. In some instances this has been corrected, as in the Cherhill Horse in Wiltshire, by the construction of a low barrier of hurdle-work along the lower edges of the figure. When last I visited the Westbury White Horse it had its outline secured by flat, up-ended stones, and drains had been inserted at the lower extremities to carry off rainwater. The Cherhill Horse, which is one of the best of the Wessex hill figures, measures 123 feet long by 131 feet high. When it was scoured a hundred years ago the work is said to have taken six men a fortnight. They raked the surface clean, then covered it with lumps of fresh chalk rammed tightly together.

Such an operation on the Cerne Giant ought not to impose any great difficulties. A spontaneous attack on it by local people, bent on enjoying themselves with such junketings as enlivened proceedings at Uffington and elsewhere in the last century is doubtless too much to hope for, though a pretext could be found should one be needed. On the hill-top 30 or 40 yards above the Giant's head and slightly to his left is a prehistoric earthen enclosure, roughly rectangular, known as The Frying Pan, and here, until some time in the nineteenth century, dancing around a maypole took place every May Day. An interesting feature of the occasion is that the maypole had to be cut and erected during the night. Anyhow, it was a good excuse for a whole-hearted village revel, and doubtless could be made so again.

Who the Giant is supposed to represent is still a matter for conjecture and debate. Some decidedly weird theories have been suggested. A local legend says that he was a Danish king who was actually that size. When invading Dorset he stretched himself out on the hillside to sleep, and the people of Cerne cut off his head and afterwards traced his outline in the turf, to commemorate the event! Probably, however, he is a pagan god, of Celtic or pre-Celtic date and therefore 2,000 or more years old. Mediaeval writers say that his name was Helith, or Helis, or Heil, or something similar, and modern writers have suggested that he was the British counterpart of Hercules. But no-one knows.

Village School Memories

Miss Packer, my first school-teacher, was a kind lady who taught me my alphabet and tables in 'the little room' of our village school. Erected in 1853, the school had bucket toilets and no wash-basins, but that was what we were used to at home, anyway. 'The little room' was a cramped apartment, screened off from 'the big room' by folding doors and heated by a tortoise slow-combustion stove. We attended school from nine to twelve and from one to half-past three, with no organised games and with very little other recreational activity that I can remember, but no-one ever escaped from that 'little room' until he had mastered the rudiments at least of reading, writing and arithmetic.

Now the politicians (it is marvellous how long they take to discover what other people have known for years) have found that a million or two youngsters are leaving school nowadays without being able to read or write or do simple sums. In most villages, the exceptions being the ones where the villagers put up a determined fight, the primary schools have been closed, and the children are taken by bus to larger schools miles away – some to one school, some to another. The schools are impressive in their architecture and equipment; the lessons are interesting; and those establishments which I have visited I have thought excellent. And yet there are these disappointing results. Can it be that the advantage Miss Packer had of not only having a small class (less than twenty of us) but of knowing all about us and our parents and families was of first importance after all? We belonged, and she belonged too, to a well-defined community. But where does a child belong now? To its family? To its village? To its school?

Mass production methods produce a standard article but sometimes at the expense of quality.

Old Christmas, 1820

As a reminder of what Christmas was like a hundred-and-sixty years ago a Stalbridge reader sent me a copy of Washington Irving's little book, *Old Christmas*, published in 1820. Irving was a celebrated American writer (he wrote, among other stories, Rip van Wynkel), who occasionally visited Europe and who here describes a Christmas he spent at an English country house.

A modern writer, skimming through the pages, is surprised at what these old-time authors got away with. Pages and pages of solid description, with words pouring out like a cascading waterfall. An efficient editor would get rid of half of them at the first reading.

Still, when one digs into the heap quite a lot of information is found, buried in the verbosity. Irving evidently moved in the higher strata of society, for in this account he is invited to spend Christmas at an English country house. There are butlers, footmen and coveys of servants, all resident in one of those houses which nowadays its harassed owner insures for a substantial sum and prays that it will be struck by lightning.

One of the points that impresses the reader is that the emphasis on religious observance at Christmas was much stronger than it is now. About sunrise Irving was woken up by three small carol-singers who were doing the rounds of the corridors, singing outside every door. Then, 'I had scarcely dressed myself,' says Irving, 'when a servant appeared to invite me to family prayers.' This country mansion had a private chapel in one wing, and by the time he had found it nearly all the rest of the household had already assembled, 'the family in a kind of gallery, furnished with cushions, hassocks and large prayer-books; the servants were seated on benches below.' The squire read the prayers, and one of the guests acted as clerk, intoning the responses. Then they sang a carol.

Almost immediately after breakfast the whole company walked half-a-mile or so through the park to the village church for another service. Here the singing was accompanied by an orchestra of violins, clarionets and bass viols, though 'accompanied' is perhaps the wrong word, for by the end of the hymn the vocalists were usually a bar or two behind the instrumentalists. The parson then preached a sermon of inordinate length, urging his congregation to be merry, which they were when eventually he desisted and let them escape.

Christmas dinner, which seems to have been taken round midday or in the early afternoon, was a gargantuan one and was preceded by a further performance by the parson, who recited a long-winded and long-worded grace. A boar's head was brought in on a silver dish, its entry being accompanied by harp music. Other meats included turkey, sirloin of beef and a pie which was adorned with peacock feathers and should have contained peacocks but which had to make do with pheasants, there having been heavy mortality among peacocks during the past season. Irving notes that old-time banquets were so lavish that three fat wethers were traditionally used 'to provide gravy for a single peacock.'

He mentions the 'Yule clog', a great log of wood which was put on the fire on Christmas Eve and was expected to burn all night. Bad luck befell the household if it went out. Huge wax tapers, decorated with greenery, were also carried into the dining-room on Christmas Eve. During Christmas Day the house received a visit from a local company of Morris dancers. After their performance they were entertained with 'brawn and beef and stout home-brewed'. And on Christmas evening a wassail bowl, 'a huge silver vessel of rare and curious workmanship', was passed round, everyone taking a drink. Its contents consisted of either ale or wine 'with nutmeg, sugar, toast, ginger and roasted crabs' (meaning crab-apples). Evidently the country house visited by Irving was not in the West Country, or the basic beverage would have been cider. The evening entertainment consisted chiefly of what seems to have been a compromise between a mumming-play and a masque, performed by the household and guests and not by visiting mummers. Among the party games played were 'hoodman blind, shoe the wild mare, hot cockles, steal the white loaf, bob-apple and snap dragon'.

It all sounds good fun, and, although the setting is a baronial hall with all the trappings of affluence, the old squire who presided over it all was convinced that something similar, though on a humbler level, was going on in every farmhouse and cottage on his estate. He may have been right. A hundred years later, in the 1920s and 1930s, we enjoyed cosy Christmasses on somewhat the same lines in our Wiltshire village. And after our private parties on Christmas Day almost the entire village would meet for an uproarious village party in the village hall on Boxing Day. In those decades of economic depression we had to manage without large expenditure, but all the food was given and we made our own entertainment, so very little money was needed.

Of course, Christmasses of the present are equally lively and gay, but there are subtle differences. One is, I think, that parties are more exclusive. They are for families, or families and friends, or for those who work in the same office or factory. For the old squire of 1820 and for us in 1930 they were community gatherings, in which everyone who lived in the neighbourhood was included. There was open house or open invitation, cutting right across social classes.

Another main difference is the amount of money spent. In 1930s there was little to spend, and the squire of the 1820s entertained his guests with mostly home-produced provisions. There were no masses of costly presents for all and sundry.

Finally, religious observance was a much more homely and personal matter. Because he and his household did so on every Sunday and saint's day throughout the year it was natural for the squire and his guests to attend an early Christmas morning service in the private chapel. When I was a boy we had family prayers every morning after breakfast. My father would read a few verses from the big family Bible, and we would all kneel down for prayers. Does anyone have family prayers now? And is England not the worse for the lapse?

Fines and Tolls

Old documents from time to time reveal surprising aspects of life in old-time villages. Not long ago a reader who spends a good deal of time digging into the archives of the West Country sent me some extracts from the Petty Sessions Records for Salisbury and Amesbury in the 1840s and 1850s, concentrating on the records concerning my native parish of Pitton and Farley, which she thought would interest me. The cases tried were mostly of poaching offences, which, of course, doesn't surprise me one bit, for nineteenth century villagers were inveterate poachers. But two unexpected entries caught my attention.

One was that in most instances one-half of the fine paid by the offender was handed over to 'the informer'. Here is a farm labourer, bearing the same surname as myself, who was found with eight pheasants' eggs in his possession on May 18th, 1851. 'Fined five shillings for each egg, together forty shillings; in default of payment to be imprisoned in the House of Correction at Fisherton Anger for one calendar month.' Then comes a signed receipt for £1, 'being moiety of the penalty imposed on the above-named George Whitlock'.

One's first impression is that forty shillings or a month in jail was a pretty stiff penalty on a farm worker with a weekly wage of probably about seven shillings. However, I note that George Whitlock was quite a regular offender, having been hauled up before the magistrates on several previous occasions. But the reference to the informer strikes a sinister note. Informers have flourished in police states and tyrannies throughout the ages, from at least the time of the Roman Empire onwards, but it comes as rather a shock to find them active in the English countryside. On reflection, I expect they were keepers, looking after their employers' business. But it must have caused severe friction in village life. Just imagine a hard-pressed cottage wife with a brood of small children, seeing five weeks' wages forfeited through the unwise activities of a feckless husband and knowing that her neighbour down the road had pocketed half of it. No wonder fights were frequent.

The other entry that intrigues, and indeed puzzles, me concerns a labourer 'convicted of being the driver but not the owner of a Waggon and two horses proceeding on the Turnpike Road at Milford on the first of December 1853 and ... thereon having no other person to guide the horses. Fined £1 and costs. In default of payment to be imprisoned in the House of Correction at Fisherton Anger for 21 days. Paid.'

It looks as though the driver of a two-horse waggon was legally obliged to have another person to lead the horses, at least on a turnpike road. The reason for such a law eludes me. And £1 (more than two weeks' wages) or three weeks in jail seems excessive.

Turnpikes are now, of course, an almost forgotten feature of the countryside, but when I was a boy the main road was always referred to in our village as 'the turnpike'. You walked two-and-a-half-miles over the downs from our valley and then came to the great highway from London to Salisbury and the West, which was 'the turnpike'. Farther on, at the bottom of a long hill, stood a little bungalow-type lodge which in times past was the residence of the turnpike-keeper. It was pulled down a few years ago, but other turnpike lodges are still quite common features of our older main roads. There must be scores of them in the West Country. Usually they are single-storied and very small, sometimes with one room on one side of the road and one on the other, and some of them represent somewhat bizarre attempts to be ornamental, with hexagonal walls, umbrella-like roofs and decorative chimneys.

Turnpikes were introduced to effect an improvement on England's roads, which until then were kept in repair by the parishes through which they passed. The job was tackled piecemeal, more than two thousand Road Acts being passed between the years 1700 and 1790. A group of country gentlemen would combine to form a turnpike trust, which, when properly established, was permitted to raise money by loan. Once this capital was invested in roads, the trust concerned was naturally permitted to erect gates or barriers across them and extract tolls from all who wanted to use them.

In the first half of last century the usual tolls were at about the following levels: – $1\frac{1}{2}$ pence for a horse; $4\frac{1}{2}$ pence for a vehicle drawn by one horse; 9 pence for a vehicle with two horses; and so on. This bore particularly severely on farmers, who often took a waggon and four horses to market. The payment of the toll entitled the vehicle to use the turnpike road till midnight, after which the driver paid again, but I gather that if a farmer returned from market with a load different from that which he took in, as would be only natural, he was generally charged a second time. And sometimes he would have to pass two or more turnpike gates on the way to town.

Once the turnpike trust had made its road and set up its barriers it would normally let out the rights of toll collection to the highest bidder. There were individuals who made a business of investing in turnpike tolls, one celebrated Manchester gentleman doing so to the reputed tune of £50,000 each year – an enormous sum in those days. He would instal a toll-collector in each lodge, at a wage of around 20 to 25 shillings a week (quite good pay in those days), and employed a troop of collectors to collect the tolls from them. Legal quarrels were commonplace, and it was said that at least half the money taken in tolls went into the pockets of lawyers, surveyors and clerks. Out of the remainder the toll-collectors had to be paid, and, of course, the roads had to be kept up. What often happened in practice was that the investors found extreme difficulty in getting any interest on their loans.

The situation became very complex. A writer at the end of the nineteenth century, recalling the turnpikes in the days of his youth, wrote that the town of Aylesbury, which he knew well, was so ringed with turnpikes that it was impossible even to take a horse outside the town to exercise without paying a toll. These turnpikes belonged to no fewer than seven independent trusts, each of which maintained its expensive set of officials. In 1840 there were 22,000 miles of turnpike roads in England, but nearly 8,000 toll gates – which meant a toll-gate at every $2\frac{3}{4}$ miles.

The whole cumbersome apparatus was eventually swept aside by the coming of the railways. Relics of the system which may still be found include not only the toll-houses but also occasional roadside signs. At St. Thomas's Bridge, on the London road a mile or so outside Salisbury, there is still (unless it has been removed very recently) an iron roadside sign informing the passerby that on one side of the central pillar was a County Bridge Road and on the other a Turnpike. And I seem to remember seeing similar turnpike notices in Dorset.

An Amesbury reader commented on the paragraph about a carter being fined, back in the 1850s, for being on a turnpike road with two horses and 'no other person to guide the horses'.

He suggested that the carter probably had 'the two horses at length, one in trace harness, and was riding on the shafts without reins on them. This was often done, as the trace horse would obey a spoken command, but it was against the law on public roads. Accidents had probably happened thorough the horses getting out of control.' He said that the law was still in force in his early days, as he remembered reading in local papers of cases in which drivers of timber carriages were fined for not having control of their team (often consisting of three or four horses). He himself was always told to put the reins on the horses when driving a farm waggon; then it was in order either to drive or to lead them.

Being summoned for drunken driving was a frequent hazard in those days, too. Coming home from market a farmer or carter would often be asleep in waggon or trap, allowing the horse to find its own way home. The police were on the alert for such behaviour, and a kind-hearted person would sometime s stop a vehicle about to enter a village and wake up the driver. Once he was awake, of course, proving he was drunk would be difficult, there being no breathalyser test!

Regarding poaching, as I mentioned in my article the fines were pretty stiff, but my correspondent says that the offender soon recouped himself, game and rabbits fetching quite good prices. But, he adds, the existence of informers led to much poaching and sheep-stealing being done by lone operators, who buried or burnt all traces of their activities. He remembers an instance or two where keepers chased a poacher almost home and then lost him among the houses. The man had to go to bed in the dark, being afraid to light a candle.

Another offence for which carters were sometimes fined was driving or riding a horse without its full quota of shoes. Some policemen, he says, would wait to check the farm teams as they came home from work in the fields. You could lead a horse, unattached to a cart, if it had lost a shoe, but, if it was in the shafts, then you were headed for trouble. Working a horse with sore shoulders also earned a fine. Not all policemen were equally zealous, however, and braces of pheasants at Christmas sometimes eased the path of the wrongdoer.

August is Unrecognisable

To me, as, I suppose, to most of my generation August is now an almost unrecognisable month. Well, we have grown used to it, but the gap between contemporary August and the August of our boyhood memories is immense.

As I write it is raining steadily, - a warm, thundery downpour descending vertically from a uniformly grey sky. So harvest is at a standstill. But life goes on normally. There are no groups of disconsolate men and women, with sacks draped like cloaks around their shoulders, standing or sitting in barns and farm sheds, waiting for the rain to stop. At the most, two or three men have had to put away their combine-harvesters and turn to another job. Tomorrow, if it is fine, they will go back to combining, with little harm done. There will be no turning of sodden sheaves, in the hope of catching some sunshine before the next storm. At the most, a few extra hours in the drier for the grain.

Just a handful of workers, well equipped with modern machinery, win the harvest. The rest of us are spectators. In the village where I now live I suppose that no more than five or six families have a direct interest in the harvest. It is, I know, primarily a dairying and stock-raising countryside here in Somerset, but at my old home in Wiltshire things are much the same. Of the ten or so remaining farmers hardly any have any permanent employees. If they don't possess a combine-harvester they hire a contractor to reap their harvest. Ten households out of, say, seventy or eighty.

Back in the 1920s, when I was a boy, there were virtually no spectators. Everybody was involved. Of the inhabitants of our village, all but a few got their living from the land. Although the number of farms was about the same, nearly all of them kept on at least one man. My father, who then had about 130 acres, employed four full-time men, if I remember rightly, plus a few pensioners who came in from time to time.

But not at harvest-time. Then every farmer grabbed whoever he could. The able-bodied men who worked for the local builder were roped in to help in the evenings. So were the shopkeeper, the blacksmith, the baker and a schoolmaster who was on holiday from his post in the city. Pensioners, boys of ten upwards and women of all ages were in demand. My father would come in exultantly to tell my mother,

'I've managed to get Old Sergeant (a retired soldier with one arm missing), and Mrs. Endicott, and those people on holiday down at Maidment's, to come and give a hand.'

No spectators. One of my earliest memories is of being pushed in a push-chair, with a can of hot tea between my little legs and a hamper of food sharing the seat, out to the harvest field, there to sit under the rick for a picnic tea with the harvesters.

'Go and turn them rooks off the hiles over the hedge,' commanded my father, and away would toddle two or three tiny tots, eager to help.

Later, it was my wife who used to bring our own children out to the harvest-field in the push-chair. History repeating itself, as it had done for many generations. But not any more.

Come to think of it, all those helpers were necessary. When we were carting sheaves to the rick we needed, – now let me see – two waggons, one being loaded in the field and one being unloaded at the rick. If we had three, so much the better, especially if there was a longish haul from field to rick. For the waggon in the field we needed two men pitching the sheaves on to it and one loading. A boy or a woman would do for the loader; but two on the load were better than one. At the rick we needed one man unloading; another in the pitch-hold; and a third passing the sheaves across to the key craftsman, the rick-maker. Say, four as a minimum, with perhaps a boy to hold the horse steady or to lead it in and out. If the boy was big enough, he could take the empty waggon out to the field and bring the full one in; but that tended to keep one or the other of the teams waiting. No, we really needed two boys. Altogether, to cart a field efficiently, a team of nine was required.

But work was probably going ahead in another field as well. Ideally, the head carter was not involved in the rick-making operation, except towards the end of the harvest. He was busy cutting the next field with the binder. And the sheaves which the binder threw out had to be stood up in stooks, or hiles as we called them, as quickly as possible. That is where the women, boys and the one-armed man came in. The more 'hilers' the better.

So, in the middle of harvest, it was easy to find work for fourteen or fifteen workers, and difficult to manage without them. During the war, when we were farming between 400 and 500 acres, we had double that number, chiefly from harvest camps. Youth groups, scouts, church organisations and others used to arrange these camps. pitch their tents under the big elms and spend a very useful if arduous holiday. Harvest was like a military campaign (and in Hitler's war almost as important as one) which lasted, with numerous setbacks, for about six weeks. And what a sense of achievement when at last we had won through.

There was some rivalry as to who would finish first. The word would go round that So-and-so has finished, and we would redouble our efforts. In old-time Devon the harvesters would stand on the highest point of the farm and shout in triumph the news that for them the harvest was ended. 'Arneck, arneck!' they shouted. 'We haven.' 'Arneck' was, I think, 'Our nack', the nack being a bunch of ears of corn from which a corn dolly was then fashioned.

Our war-time harvests culminated in an improptu concert around a camp-fire, with barbecues going (although we did not then know that word). And many of those who participated still testify that those were some of the happiest days of their lives.

In the Somerset parish where I live at present it is still possible to trace, in more than one field, the mediaeval 'baulks' into which the open fields were divided. They are a series of parallel and rounded ridges a few yards across. Each baulk was cultivated by a different peasant, for the general rule was that no peasant should have two adjoining, though he might hold a dozen or two in different parts of the parish. So we can imagine the August scene of five or six hundred years ago, the fields alive with peasants, the men mowing with scythe or sickle, the women gathering the sheaves for tying, the children gleaning, or driving birds away and looking after tinier ones. Everyone involved in the harvest, and knowing that on it depended their living in the coming winter.

From that scene to the one I remember in the 1920s and indeed the 1940s is only a short step. We would have recognised those mediaeval peasants, and they us. But between the 1940s and the 1970s gapes an immeasurable gulf. It seems incredible that one human life can span it. And when my generation has gone a door will be shut on a way of life which even now our grandchildren find impossible to imagine. A wet August will mean nothing more than a spoilt holiday.

The Ooser

In April, 1978, I was privileged to see an Ooser mask. A newly-made one, it is true, but painstakingly and skilfully fashioned to the pattern of the West Country's last-known Ooser mask, which disappeared from Melbury Osmund about the turn of the century. Fortunately a photograph of the Melbury Ooser survives, and this modern one resembled it almost exactly. It was made of wood, with whiskers of wool from Jacob sheep, a ruddy complexion, huge staring eyes and a splendid pair of bull's horns. The lower jaw was moveable, each motion revealing a double set of gleaming teeth. The only point of difference was that the original mask was intended to be worn by a man, whereas this one was mounted on a metal and wooden stand and was to be carried in procession, on a pole.

And what, many readers may ask, is an Ooser? Well, I used to wonder when I was a boy and my father would say, jokingly,

'Come on now, or the Ooser'll have 'ee!'

That was in south Wiltshire, too, and most traditions associate the Ooser with Dorset.

It is said that most Dorset villages once had an Ooser mask. It was worn by a local man on such occasions as club festivals, Christmas celebrations, coronations and similar festivities, or, in some places, for no special occasions at all except as an excuse for parading around the village asking for beer money. The wearer capered about and bellowed alarmingly, as he was supposed to, for he was meant to be a terrifying object.

He was, in fact, the old pagan horned god, the god who was represented by the wild bull of the forest. He was a god of fertility. In far-off pre-Christian times the mask would have been worn by the priest of a tribe, in fertility rites of the ancient religion. In particular he was associated with May Day, and it is not impossible that he had connections with the Cerne Abbas giant, around which May Day revels were held as late as the nineteenth century.

Like other pagan gods, he was relegated by Christian missionaries to the status of a devil. As his hold on people's minds was too strong for him to be abolished, he was made to appear as evil as possible. In some instances he appeared as a dragon in old mumming plays.

In the later stages of his career he seems to have become associated with the custom of skimmetting, of which perhaps the best known example is in Thomas Hardy's *The Mayor of Casterbridge*. Here the object was to expose to shame a man or woman accused of adultery, cruelty to a marital partner, or some similar irregularity. It was perhaps appropriate that the Ooser should put in an appearance, seeing that sexual misconduct was usually alleged. Skimmetting, incidentally, was a custom once widespread in Wessex and certainly not confined to Dorset.

So now, after seventy or eighty years, Dorset has an Ooser again. This modern specimen was made at Holwell, near Sherborne, for a Mediaeval Fair being held there, appropriately enough, on May Day. I later learned that an earlier Ooser was made for a meeting of the Morris Ring of England (an organisation of Morris dancers) in September, 1973. John Byfleet of Weymouth, the maker, went to endless trouble to get all the details right, first making a model of papier maché and then carving the final mask from solid wood.

This Weymouth Ooser was considerably larger than the Holwell one, for, with the frame that fitted over the shoulders of the bearer, it weighed 28 pounds. The colours with which it was painted were mixed with animal blood, as those of the original Oosers probably were. And the bearer had a mantle of cured cow skin draped over him. At all costs he had to remain anonymous; when he donned or discarded the mask he went to cover behind a building and was screened from sight by his companions. The Weymouth Ooser stood about eight feet high, the bearer peeping out from a hole in his neck. In spite of the weight of the mask, it was nicely balanced, and a man who had worn it told me he was able to do so for an hour or more and to caper about quite vigorously all the time.

I hopped out of bed wide awake just after six o'clock on May Day morning and began to dress, humming the May Day tune.

'Where are you off to?' asked my wife, drowsily, from the pillow.

'I think I'll go down to Cerne Abbas and watch the Morris men dance on Giant's Hill,' I said.

I think I heard a muffled 'Fool!' from under the blankets.

The cuckoo was calling outside the window, so, to match its

mood, I sang the words of the song that had been going through
my head – the old May Day round we learned at primary school
in Wiltshire.

'May Day's breaking,
All the world's awaking,
Let us see the sun rise
Over the Plain.
Why have you awoke me?
How you do provoke me?
Let me have a little time
To doze off again.
Sleeping in the daytime
Wastes the happy Maytime,
Makes an empty pocket and a cloudy brain.'

But it was lost on my wife, who was now fast asleep again.

At Cerne Abbas the Wessex Morris dancers were assembling,
and I marvelled at the hardihood of the characters who lugged
the heavy Ooser to the top of the steep Giant's Hill. Both The
Giant and the Frying Pan (the earthwork above it) are now out of
bounds, protected by a barbed wire fence because of erosion, so
the dancers performed a little higher up the hill. Although it was
still only half-past seven on a misty morning, somewhere around a
hundred spectators arrived.

The Morris men performed energetically, and the Ooser, with
renewed vigour pranced around. Towering two feet above the
heads of the tallest men present he was in his true environment – a
grim and menacing figure in the mist. Here was the authentic
bogeyman of which our ancestors spoke. Although we were about
so early in the morning, on oldtime May Days the dance would
have been performed even earlier, probably at daybreak, while
the light was still very dim. As a representation of the old horned
god, the Ooser would, with a few theatrical aids, have been really
awe-inspiring.

The Morris men themselves are the heirs of a very ancient
tradition, having been in times past a kind of secret society for
men only, but their costumes are not as ancient as their cult. The
knee-breeches, open-necked shirts, jerkins and straw hats
evidently date from about the time of Nelson, or not much earlier.
It would have been interesting to see them, for the Cerne Abbas
occasion, wearing skins and costumes to match the Ooser's. The
sinister effect would have undoubtedly been heightened.

Back down in Cerne Abbas the dancers lined up and danced in procession to the square, where they danced with a vigour which I wished I could emulate at that time in the morning for about half-an-hour. In pouring rain too. And hardly any of the spectators owned defeat by the weather and went home.

Then into the Royal Oak for a welcome breakfast of eggs, bacon, sausages and coffee, while saturated shirts were dried out before a log fire.

Abbotsbury, said the Morris men, was to be the next stop, but I had an engagement about noon at Holwell, where the other resurrected Dorset Ooser lives. Holwell, near Sherborne, had organised a mediaeval May Fair, and my wife and I were to judge the mediaeval costumes. Unfortunately, in defiance of an optimistic weather forecast (and how exasperated I get with the weather forecasters when they fail to apologise for getting a forecast hopelessly wrong, as they did on May Day), the rain had now settled in for a steady downpour. It was a great pity, for Holwell is a delightful little village,- the perfect setting for the festivities which were planned.

Many of the scheduled items went ahead in the rain. The Mayor was installed, the Town Crier (from Yetminster and in splendid voice) shouted his proclamations, the May Queen was crowned and the procession processed around the village. But the Mumming Play, and the Maypole dancing and the pony-and-trap marathon had to be abandoned.

But never have I been more impressed by the cheerfulness of a community in adversity. Cheerful faces everywhere; no real despondency; everyone making the best of a situation that could have been most depressing. Good for Holwell. The right good cheer extended even to the characters, soaked to the skin, who had to manhandle virtually every car out of the meadow used as a car park.

One feature of the day struck an authentic mediaeval note. The village church became the natural refuge from the rain and a focus for as many events as possible. This is where my wife and I judged the costumes, while many of the villagers sat around in the pews with their picnic baskets and munched sandwiches. Afterwards, while we had lunch in the parlour of a devoted lady whose house seemed to be open to all comers, country dancing and other events went ahead in the church. This is undoubtedly how parish churches were used in the days of Merrie England.

Hard Wiltshire Cheese

An old friend of mine at West Moors came across some notes made by someone touring Wiltshire in 1871 and was puzzled by the following reference.

'It is surely the most vitalising wind that breaks over England; and if it were not for the hard Wiltshire beer and the still harder cheese, one hardly knows how any Wiltshiremen could contrive to die short of a hundred years.'

What was wrong with this hard beer and cheese? she asks. She had asked several Wiltshiremen, and they can't understand it.

Well, this Wiltshireman can. At least, about the cheese, if not the beer. The sort of cheese which farm labourers ate was made from skimmed milk and was as hard as concrete. A story I once heard about a gipsy woman who, begging at the door of a Wiltshire farmhouse, was given a hunk of this cheese, illustrates its character.

After examining it she turned to the housewife and enquired innocently, 'Do you suffer from bad eyesight, ma'am?'

'Why, yes,' admitted the good lady. 'My eyes aren't as good as they used to be.'

'Well,' said the gipsy, 'you toast this cheese, and the first drop of fat which falls from it, catch it and rub it on your eyes. That'll cure them. It would cure anything!'

Long Barrows

On a windy but fortunately fine morning just before Easter we climbed to the top of a Cotswold hill, just short of 1000 feet above sea level, to see the great long barrow of Belas Knap. It was, of course, not necessary to travel to the Cotswolds to find long barrows; there are many in Wessex, including no fewer than ten within a couple of miles of Stonehenge, and another five near Avebury. However, Belas Knap is a particularly large and imposing specimen and, when excavated in 1863, proved to contain 38 burials.

Long barrows are neolithic earthworks estimated to date from 3000 to 1800 B.C. Some of them are larger than the average house, and the biggest are a hundred yards long. And a house is evidently what they originally were – a house of the dead. It was a long, narrow house, with walls of hurdle-work or timber, filled in with chalk or clay or whatever material happened to be available locally. It contained a central corridor, along either sides of which were burial chambers, much as in a family vault. Evidently most long barrows were used over a considerable period of time, serving a princely family for a number of generations. In most instances there was an enclosure at the entrance, where religious ceremonies were probably held. Archaeologists think that the corpses were first exposed, perhaps to the activities of carnivorous birds, as on the 'towers of silence' in the East, the bones being gathered up for interment later.

When eventually the charnel house was sealed and abandoned, the timber or wattlework would in due course decay, allowing the filling to spread and settle, thus forming the long low mound we now see. The Belas Knap barrow, though now sealed, has its entrance and some other recesses still exposed, showing how it is beautifully constructed with thin Cotswold stones, such as those used for roofing tiles. It seems that later people dug holes in its sides for their own burials.

Many long barrows were excavated in the middle years of the nineteenth century but some remained untouched, and where these are situated in places where they are unlikely to be disturbed by modern 'development' or by agriculture they are being allowed to remain as they are, waiting for investigation by some later age with perhaps better methods of archaeology than ours.

The Twelve Days of Christmas

It is interesting to remind ourselves that a fortnight's holiday at Christmas is no new thing. In mediaeval England it was apparently standard practice. Do you remember the Twelve Days of Christmas in the carol? They were twelve days of holiday. Twelfth Night marked the official end of the Christmas holiday, and is still remembered today as the date when housewives take down the Christmas decorations.

Much depends, of course, on what one means by a holiday. Most of our ancestors in those days were peasants, and on the farm there are chores to be done, come Sunday, Bank Holiday, Christmas or any other festival. The animals have to be fed and given fresh litter; the cows have to be milked; calving cows have to be attended to. In the old days, water had to be drawn from the well, and the wood-pile replenished. Indoors any housewife will testify that there is no respite from cleaning, preparing meals, washing up and attending to the needs of the children.

What else, then, *was* there for the peasant to do in the middle of winter? The answer is, Work in the fields – ploughing, hauling and spreading farmyard manure, hedging, ditching. These were the tasks which were abandoned in the Twelve Days of Christmas. Then, on Twelfth Night, there was a fine beano, with dancing, feasting, folk plays and bonfires, also including wassailing the apple-trees. Wassailing is now carried out on or as near as possible to January 16th, that being Old Twelfth Night – allowing for the loss of eleven days due to the calendar change in 1752.

Nor is that all. The Monday after Twelfth Night was Plough Monday. The plough was brought out of its shed and blessed, preparatory to beginning its work for the year. Again there was dancing and mumming and a feast of sorts. The late Rolf Gardiner of Fontmell attempted to revive some of the old Plough Monday customs, and it was a pity that the outbreak of war halted the experiment, for it was catching on very well.

But what really intrigues me about all this is the fact that our ancestors considered the beginning of the year's work an occasion for festivity and rejoicing. To make the return to work after a holiday a celebration is really an unfamiliar attitude in this century. Though perhaps some of the frustrated unemployed, who would like a job but cannot get one, would understand.

Limited Access

In a Somerset town I went through a house into the garden and was inspecting some old buildings, including a bakery, when the owner pointed out one which was a stable. It was where the horse which pulled the bread-van lived.

'But how did he get in and out?' I asked, not seeing any obvious access.

'Same way as you did, – through the house!' he said.

And that, I think, was a fairly common arrangement in the old days, where terraced houses were concerned. I remember that a few years ago a householder in the Isle of Purbeck told me he could remember when the cow was taken through the passage in the middle of the house, to graze on a plot of grass at the back. Someone walked behind with a stick, to discourage her from dropping anything until she was safely outside.

A Village in 1851

A Chichester (Sussex) reader who knows, as probably many of my readers know, that I was born in and have spent much of my life in the village of Pitton, near Salisbury, thoughtfully sent me photocopies of the details of the entries for Pitton in the census of 1851. This is the first time I have seen such a comprehensive record of the village in the middle of the nineteenth century, and naturally I find it fascinating. Here is my paternal grandfather, about the mystery of whose death I wove my book *A Family and a Village*, but he is a boy of nine. Here is James Barnett, another ancestor of mine, who was the village shoemaker and whose four daughters had to take turns in getting up at half-past four in the morning to read the Bible to their father for four hours to keep him awake while he worked till breakfast-time. Here is Mark Collins, a child of one year, whose widow I remember as a very old lady when I was a boy. And many others.

It is, of course, in this respect of more interest to myself who have a personal link with the persons whose names are recorded, but when I came to look more closely into the records and to analyse them some facts emerge of more general interest. Some confirm commonly held impressions of life in a mid-nineteenth century village but some completely contradict them.

There were 97 occupied houses and 2 unoccupied. The population was 312, which works out at only just over three persons per house. That is so much less than is generally supposed that I looked into the size of the families. We think of large Victorian families of twelve or thirteen children, but in this census I found none of those. The largest number of children per family was seven, and there was only one family of that size.

I made a list of all families which consisted of married couples aged between 20 and 55, which is the age-group which would be likely to have all their children at home. 10 had no children; 12 had one child; 12 had two children; 19 had three; 8 had four; 5 had five; 4 had six; and one had seven. The totals are 181 children for 71 families. Which works out at an average of 2.56 children per family and is not much different from the present average, I believe. Moreover, the children in most families were often quite widely spaced – not one per year.

Of course, it may be that many more were born and died early. To determine that, one would need to compare the census with the births and deaths register. I do notice that there are no fewer than nine widowers in the prime of life – say, from 25 to 45, which indicates a higher mortality rate than now prevails among the mothers.

I noticed another odd fact. Out of the 70 married couples (of all ages) recorded, no fewer than 19 of the wives were older than their husbands. I wonder why? It seems an unusually high proportion.

There are twelve spinsters over the age of 21 living with their parents, some of them evidently keeping house for a brother or a widowed father, though one old lady, Christina Webb, who says she is a retired farmer, has three unmarried daughters in their twenties living at home. One suspects a dragon of a matron who thinks the local lads aren't good enough for her daughters.

The village has ten bachelors over the age of 21.

I was interested to discover what the educational situation was. The primary school that still functions admirably was founded in 1853, two years after this census, but the village had a school in 1851. A lady, Elizabeth Williams, aged 43 and without children of her own, is registered as a schoolmistress. Her husband is an agricultural worker. She has an assistant a sixteen-year-old girl, daughter of a widow. My father remembered having been told that, before the school was built, there used to be what he called a 'dame's school', and he knew which house it was held in.

30 children are entered in the census as scholars. The attitude of the various families towards education evidently varies considerably. Here is a journeyman bricklayer, Joshua Collins, who has a daughter aged thirteen still at school. But here is an agricultural labourer, William Collins, whose son Samuel, aged eleven, is already at work on the farm. There are quite a number of boys aged thirteen and fourteen entered as agricultural labourers. Rather surprisingly, there are more girls than boys of eleven and over at school. Yet a generation earlier the parish register, of marriages, shows that it is the girls who are illiterate.

It is not necessarily the labourers' children who are absent from school and the better-off ones who attend. John Seward is a farmer of 132 acres, employing 4 men and with three daughters aged 5 to 10, none of whom go to school. Samuel Cooke, a sawyer, has 6 children, 4 of school age, but none attend school. On the other hand, several agricultural labourers have children at school, though three is the maximum number per family. Probably they had to pay a penny a week per child, and threepence was the maximum they could afford. In the cottages by Pitton Green, where the sun shines only in the afternoon because of the shadowing hill and where the poorer families lived, there are twenty-two children of school age, not one of whom goes to school.

The village is fairly self-contained. Of the 312 inhabitants, 219 were born in the village. 12 of the others were born in Clarendon Park, adjoining the village fields, 19 in Winterslow and 6 in Farley, the neighbouring villages. Of the others, 29 were born within six miles of the place. That leaves only 27 who have come to reside in the village from more distant places, and most of those are from Wiltshire or Hampshire villages not far away. Several of these are listed as wives, and my guess is that they would be girls who were in service at nearby Clarendon House and had met their husbands at local functions.

As regards occupations, 91 men and boys are classified as agricultural labourers. There are 10 woodmen and one hurdle-maker, though probably some of the woodmen also made hurdles. The village had 6 farmers, one of whom was a boy of nineteen. Of the 11 carpenters, 2 were master carpenters and 9 journeymen carpenters (employed presumably at day rates); there were also 2 sawyers and 3 bricklayers. The village had one blacksmith, one brushmaker (a boy of sixteen), three shoemakers (one of whom describes himself by the now obsolete term, 'cordwainer') and an innkeeper, Stephen Offer, who has his 23-year-old sister-in-law as a barmaid. I am surprised to see three wood-turners, a craft not represented in Pitton within the past hundred years. On the other hand, there is no carrier, no master-builder and, according to the census, no shopkeeper. A 46-years-old man with two small children is described as a pensioner and agricultural labourer; presumably he received a pension from the Army. There is one other pensioner, a man of 79 who is also recorded as a visitor. The village has only one person recorded as a pauper, and she is an old lady of 75 who is living with her son-in-law.

Several of the cottagers but none of the farmers have single yong men living in. The master carpenter has one resident apprentice and one young journeyman carpenter under his roof. There are not many men of over 70, but one old chap of 78 is listed as an agricultural labourer and so is presumably still at work.

Later, two or three readers asked whether such details are readily available for other villages and for other years. The situation, as I understand it, is this:-

Censuses were taken at ten yearly intervals starting in 1801. The early ones, however, recorded only numbers of persons per family or per household, not names. The first census to provide details of every person in every family was that of 1851, and the ten-yearly censuses after that date followed the new pattern. So there is a pretty complete record from 1851 onwards, but not before.

What I saw was a photo-copy of the Enumerator's sheets in his own handwriting. Presumably an official visited each village on the appointed day and went around from house to house, checking on the inhabitants; or else he established an office in somebody's house and required the householders to come to him. I rather think that the first method must have been the one adopted, for here and there I can trace the sequence of houses visited in our village.

I believe that for Wiltshire, and probably for other western counties the enumerators' records are kept in the Public Record Office, where no doubt this photo-copy was taken.

It is intriguing to visualize the Enumerator arriving at the village on that morning (spring or summer, I think), 125 years ago. No doubt for Pitton, the village with which I am here concerned, he would jog out from Salisbury by pony and trap or by hackney carriage. The novelty of the occasion must have given rise to much discussion among the villagers, and no doubt some of them considered it outrageous that the Government should want to know all those details about everybody. The wiseacres would shake their heads. More taxes, or something equally bad, they would prophesy.

For those of us who are interested in the past, it is fascinating to have what is, in effect, a detailed verbal photograph of our ancestral village on that morning. I find it even more so when I can identify some of the characters and know what happened to them subsequently.

Here, for instance, is young Abraham Collins, aged 24, and his wife, Sarah, aged 22, not long married. Next autumn, in early October, he will be playing cricket in a closely-contested match between Pitton and the neighbouring village, Farley, in a field about midway between the two. Who won is not recorded, but we know that Abraham was called to rush home before the barrel of beer, the trophy claimed by the winning team, was broached because his wife had produced their first baby.

Here is Henry Maton, at the age of 19 the biggest farmer in the village, cultivating 320 acres and employing 12 labourers. He lives with his unmarried sister, Thirzah, aged 23. Both were born in the village, and one imagines that they had lost their parents not long before. We know that on a March day ten or twelve years later a catastrophic fire will consume his farm, his barns and buildings, his ricks, his neighbour's farm and buildings and a number of cottages. Fanned by a strong north-east wind the fire will send flames leaping high in the air, and sparks will fall in Salisbury, five miles away as the crow flies. Henry Maton will be so discouraged that he will sell up what remains of his property and emigrate to Australia.

It will be established that the fire started in a certain barn, up-wind from the farmsteads. It is said that boys were playing there at the time and were presumably responsible. Suspicion falls on certain boys, one of whom is young Arthur, whom I remember as my great-uncle. But nothing is ever proved against them. In the 1851 census Arthur is a little innocent, aged seven months, the first child of 27-year-old Charles and his 20-year-old mother, Charlotte.

Then there is my great-grandfather, William, a widower aged

35, living with his son, Daniel, aged 9, and his two daughters, Phillida, aged 5, and Susannah, aged 3. His niece, Tirza Noyce, is keeping house for him. We know that he will later marry again and will have more children and that his first family will not get on too well with their stepmother. We know that, in his old age, too old for regular farm work, he will set up business on his own account as an ash-collector, going around the villages with a donkey-cart and collecting ashes for sale to farmers as manure. There will be an occasion when the hollow elm in which he stores his ashes will catch fire one Sunday morning, giving children a glorious excuse to play truant from Sunday School. And one day he will be found dead, sitting in the little house at the end of the garden.

As for young Daniel, he will be a trumpeter in the village band. He will marry his cousin, Jane Noyce, from Winterslow, and will die of pneumonia, brought on by exposure, in his early thirties, leaving a family of three small children. Of his sisters, Susannah will die young, but Phillida will go with her husband, James Parsons, to Canada, there to establish a farm on the present site of Calgary airport.

Arthur Parsons, a young married man of 27, will succeed in due course to his father's farm and will live there all his life. Jabez Laversuch, recorded as an agricultural labourer, will presently open a village shop. Of John Seward's large family it will be his younger son, Stephen, who will succeed to his 132-acre farm. Emma Whitlock, a 16-year-old girl living with her widowed mother and helping at the dame's school, will in three years' time marry young Charles Fry, a farm worker. And we can pair off young Joshua White, aged 9, and Julia Barnett, aged 5, who will later marry and become my grandparents.

So the Enumerator, having recorded 97 households and about 300 persons, closed his book, flexed his aching wrist and climbed into his carriage preparatory to the long drive back to Salisbury. And the village, having been captured in his pages for a fleeting moment on that summer day, went about its work again and forgot him. And we look at the villagers as though we were looking at characters in a play.

It gives me an odd feeling to identify them and to think, Well, I know what's going to happen to you, although you don't. At the back of my mind is the uneasy query, I wonder whether somebody is watching me like that ... now!

In my previous notes I made the point that in a rather large number of households, the wives were older than their husbands. A correspondent who had engaged in some similar research told me he was struck by the number of widows in mid-19th century probate inventories in Dorset. He came to the conclusion that many of these could be second or third wives, and he visualized the sequence of affairs as follows. The first wife dies, perhaps in childbirth, and the husband marries again, a much younger woman. She naturally outlives him and inherits his property, which makes her an object of interest to a younger man, who duly becomes her second husband.

It seems likely enough. I was rather intrigued to find an instance of a widow, shown in the 1851 census as a cottager, possessing property valued at £400. This seems little by our standards, but as, at that time, one could acquire a neat little cottage for £25, she could have been the owner of some sixteen houses. Say the best part of £200,000 by present-day values. Phew!